D1639650

BIRDS IN COLOUR

BIRDS IN COLOUR

ILLUSTRATED BY
KARL AAGE TINGGAARD

WITH DESCRIPTIONS BY
BRUCE CAMPBELL

BLANDFORD PRESS
POOLE DORSET

First published by Penguin Books in 1960

—

Text copyright © Bruce Campbell, 1960

Revised edition April 1966
published by Blandford Press Ltd.,
Link House, West Street, Poole,
Dorset BH15 1LL
second revised edition Dec. 1968
third revised edition 1971
fourth revised edition 1974
Reprinted 1979

ISBN 0 7137 0672 4

Printed in Singapore by Toppan Printing Co. (S) Pte. Ltd.

CONTENTS

FOREWORD

THE *coloured pictures of Birds in this book were drawn by a Danish artist, Karl Aage Tinggaard, and were originally published in Sweden and Denmark under the title* Fåglarna i Färg *and* Fugle i Farver *respectively. The accompanying descriptions were written by Sigfrid Durango (Sweden) and Hans Hvass (Denmark).*

Owing to differences between the fauna of Scandinavia and Britain, it has been necessary to replace some of the original subjects by British species. New illustrations for these have been supplied by the artist.

It is hoped that this book will help those who go about in the towns, in the country and by the sea in the British Isles – and those who look observantly out of their kitchen windows – to recognize the birds they see and so add pleasure to their holiday and to their daily round. About 470 different kinds of birds have now been recorded in the British Isles; this book deals with over 250 of those most likely to be met and includes all those which breed regularly and nearly all those which breed occasionally with us, as well as the commoner winter visitors and passage migrants.

I am pleased to join my friends Sigfrid Durango and Hans Hvass in providing a text to support the beautiful paintings of Karl Aage Tinggaard.

BRUCE CAMPBELL

October 1973

CLASSIFICATION

ALL animals and plants are arranged in a certain scientific order, which unfortunately keeps being changed for reasons excellent in themselves but most annoying to the ordinary observer. Birds are now supposed to be arranged in the 'Peters-Gadow' classification. But both the five-volume *Handbook of British Birds* (1938–41) and Dr D.A. Bannerman's even larger work follow the older 'Hartert' classification. Because these continue to be the main books of reference for British bird-watchers, and because I think the Hartert order is much more practical for this country, I have followed it rather freely in this book, making slight alterations so that similar birds can appear as far as possible at the same page opening.

As regards the details of classification, the Class Aves is broken down into two Sub-classes, each containing Orders. Orders are divided into Families, Families into Genera, and each Genus is composed of Species, which are the basic biological units, though they may be further divided into Sub-species or geographical Races. I have interrupted the descriptions of species by short general sections on each Order. I have divided the great Order Passeriformes (perching birds) into its Families, and the Order Charadriiformes into its three distinct Sub-orders. A few distinctive Races are given separate headings (e.g. 40, 41 and 42, 43) and others are referred to in the text. But I have not mentioned all the British Races, as many of them cannot be told apart in the field.

THE DESCRIPTIONS

Every ornithologist has his own ideas on how to identify birds, but everyone in Britain acknowledges his debt to the *Handbook of British Birds* already mentioned, the storehouse of the pooled experience of British bird-watchers, transmuted by its team of gifted editors. I have consulted freely the sections on 'Field Characters and General Habits', compiled for each bird with such unerring felicity by the late B. W. Tucker. In many cases his succinct descriptions cannot be improved upon, but I have tried as far as possible to provide alternatives.

Each bird is described under the number given it in the coloured plates; information is given only to supplement the plates and help recognition in the field. I have avoided nearly all technical terms.

After the number comes the English name in general use to-day and the scientific generic and specific names used in *A Species List of British and Irish Birds* (1971), published by the British Trust for Ornithology.

The first sentences cover status, distribution, and habitat *in the British Isles*, some knowledge of which helps when you see a bird you do not know. The Channel Isles, which belong zoologically to France, are not included except for a note under 45.

DESCRIPTION. Details obvious from the plate are not repeated and references are given to the flight sketches of certain Orders on pages 221-3. The length in inches is quoted from *The Handbook of British Birds*. Points of difference from similar-looking birds are given where useful; also brief remarks on female, juvenile, immature, and winter plumages not shown in the plate.

VOICE. Only the commonest calls and the song are described.

HABITS. Information on stance, gait, feeding methods, flight, flocking, and roosting which may aid identification. Nesting is not covered.

MAY BE CONFUSED. Under this heading follow the numbers, in this book, of birds with which confusion is possible under reasonable conditions of observation.

If a section is omitted, it means that no useful information under it can be given; for example, some winter visitors are silent in Britain so VOICE is omitted in their case.

The conventional signs ♂ = male and ♀ = female are used on the coloured plates.

1. RAVEN, *Corvus corax*

2. HOODED CROW, *Corvus corone cornix*

3. CARRION CROW, *Corvus corone corone*

4. ROOK, *Corvus frugilegus*

5. JACKDAW, *Corvus monedula*

6. MAGPIE, *Pica pica*

7. Jay, *Garrulus glandarius*

8. Chough, *Pyrrhocorax pyrrhocorax*

9. STARLING, *Sturnus vulgaris*

10. GOLDEN ORIOLE, *Oriolus oriolus* ♂

11. HAWFINCH, *Coccothraustes coccothraustes*

12. GREENFINCH, *Carduelis chloris*

13. GOLDFINCH, *Carduelis carduelis*

14. SISKIN, *Carduelis spinus* ♀ ♂

15. REDPOLL, *Acanthis flammea*
♂ above, ♀

16. TWITE, *Acanthis flavirostris*

17. LINNET, *Acanthis cannabina* ♂

18. BULLFINCH, *Pyrrhula pyrrhula* ♂ ♀

19. SCARLET ROSEFINCH, *Carpodacus erythrinus* ♂

20. CROSSBILL, *Loxia curvirostra* ♀ ♂

21. CHAFFINCH, *Fringilla coelebs* ♂ ♀

22. BRAMBLING, *Fringilla montifringilla* ♂

23. CORN BUNTING, *Emberiza calandra*

25. YELLOWHAMMER
Emberiza citrinella ♂

24. ORTOLAN, *Emberiza hortulana* ♂

26. CIRL BUNTING, *Emberiza cirlus* ♂ ♀

27. REED BUNTING, *Emberiza schoeniclus* ♂ ♀

28. Lapland Bunting, *Calcarius lapponicus* ♂ summer

29. Snow Bunting, *Plectrophenax nivalis* ♂ summer

30. HOUSE SPARROW, *Passer domesticus* ♀ ♂

31. TREE SPARROW, *Passer montanus*

32. WOODLARK, *Lullula arborea*

33. SKYLARK, *Alauda arvensis*

34. SHORELARK, *Eremophila alpestris*

35. TAWNY PIPIT, *Anthus campestris*

36. TREE PIPIT, *Anthus trivialis*

37. MEADOW PIPIT, *Anthus pratensis*

38. ROCK PIPIT, *Anthus spinoletta*

39. GREY WAGTAIL, *Motacilla cinerea* ♂

40. BLUE-HEADED WAGTAIL, *Motacilla flava flava* ♂
(Black-headed Wagtail ♂ behind)

41. YELLOW WAGTAIL, *Motacilla flava flavissima* ♀ ♂

42. WHITE WAGTAIL, *Motacilla alba alba*

43. PIED WAGTAIL, *Motacilla alba yarrellii* ♂ ♀

44. NUTHATCH, *Sitta europaea*

45. TREECREEPER, *Certhia familiaris*

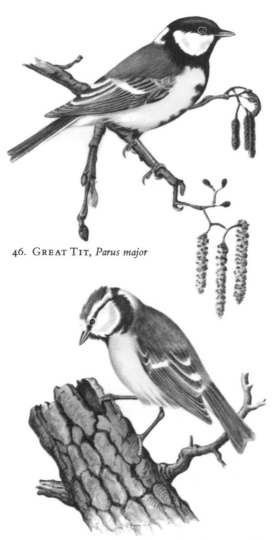

46. GREAT TIT, *Parus major*

47. BLUE TIT, *Parus caeruleus*

48. COAL TIT, *Parus ater*

49. CRESTED TIT, *Parus cristatus*

50. MARSH TIT, *Parus palustris*

51. WILLOW TIT, *Parus montanus*

52. Long-tailed Tit, *Aegithalos caudatus*

53. Bearded Tit or Reedling, *Panurus biarmicus*
♂ above, ♀

54. GREAT GREY SHRIKE, *Lanius excubitor*

55. RED-BACKED SHRIKE, *Lanius collurio* ♂

56. Waxwing, *Bombycilla garrulus*

57. Spotted Flycatcher, *Muscicapa striata*

58. PIED FLYCATCHER, *Ficedula hypoleuca* ♀ ♂

59. RED-BREASTED FLYCATCHER, *Ficedula parva* ♂

60. GOLDCREST, *Regulus regulus* ♂

61. FIRECREST, *Regulus ignicapillus*

62. CHIFFCHAFF, *Phylloscopus collybita*

63. WILLOW WARBLER, *Phylloscopus trochilus*

64. WOOD WARBLER, *Phylloscopus sibilatrix*

65. YELLOW-BROWED WARBLER, *Phylloscopus inornatus*

66. GRASSHOPPER WARBLER, *Locustella naevia*

67. SEDGE WARBLER, *Acrocephalus schoenobaenus*

68. REED WARBLER, *Acrocephalus scirpaceus*

69. MARSH WARBLER, *Acrocephalus palustris*

70. ICTERINE WARBLER, *Hippolais icterina*

71. DARTFORD WARBLER, *Sylvia undata* ♂

72. Barred Warbler, *Sylvia nisoria*

73. Garden Warbler, *Sylvia borin*

74. Blackcap, *Sylvia atricapilla* ♂ ♀

75. COMMON WHITETHROAT, *Sylvia communis*

76. LESSER WHITETHROAT, *Sylvia curruca*

77. FIELDFARE, *Turdus pilaris*

78. MISTLE THRUSH, *Turdus viscivorus*

79. Song Thrush, *Turdus philomelos*

80. Redwing, *Turdus iliacus*

81. Ring Ouzel, *Turdus torquatus* ♂

82. Blackbird, *Turdus merula* ♀ above, ♂

83. WHEATEAR, *Oenanthe oenanthe* ♂

84. WHINCHAT, *Saxicola rubetra* ♂

85. STONECHAT, *Saxicola torquata* ♂ above, ♀

86. REDSTART, *Phoenicurus phoenicurus* ♂ ♀

87. BLACK REDSTART, *Phoenicurus ochruros* ♂

88. NIGHTINGALE, *Luscinia megarhynchos*

89. ROBIN, *Erithacus rubecula*

90. DUNNOCK OR HEDGE SPARROW, *Prunella modularis*

91. WREN, *Troglodytes troglodytes*

92. DIPPER, *Cinclus cinclus*

93. SWALLOW, *Hirundo rustica*

94. HOUSE MARTIN, *Delichon urbica*

95. SAND MARTIN, *Riparia riparia*

96. Swift, *Apus apus*

97. Nightjar, *Caprimulgus europaeus*

98. HOOPOE, *Upupa epops*

99. ROLLER, *Coracias garrulus*

100. KINGFISHER, *Alcedo atthis*

101. Green Woodpecker, *Picus viridis*

102. Lesser Spotted Woodpecker, *Dendrocopos minor* ♂

103. GREAT SPOTTED WOODPECKER, *Dendrocopos major* ♂ ♀

104. WRYNECK, *Jynx torquilla*

105. CUCKOO, *Cuculus canorus*, male and 'hepatic' female

106. SNOWY OWL, *Nyctea scandiaca* ♀

107. LITTLE OWL, *Athene noctua*

108. LONG-EARED OWL, *Asio otus*

109. SHORT-EARED OWL, *Asio flammeus*

110. Tawny Owl, *Strix aluco*

111. Barn Owl, *Tyto alba*

112. KESTREL, *Falco tinnunculus* ♂

113. PEREGRINE, *Falco peregrinus*

114. HOBBY, *Falco subbuteo*

115. MERLIN, *Falco columbarius* ♂

116. GOLDEN EAGLE, *Aquila chrysaetos*

117. ROUGH-LEGGED BUZZARD
Buteo lagopus

118. COMMON BUZZARD, *Buteo buteo*

119. MARSH HARRIER, *Circus aeruginosus* ♀ above, ♂

120. MONTAGU'S HARRIER, *Circus pygargus* ♀ above, ♂

121. HEN HARRIER, *Circus cyaneus* ♀ ♂

122. GOSHAWK, *Accipiter gentilis*

123. SPARROWHAWK, *Accipiter nisus* ♀

124. RED KITE, *Milvus milvus*

125. SEA EAGLE, *Haliaeetus albicilla*

126. HONEY BUZZARD, *Pernis apivorus*

127. OSPREY, *Pandion haliaetus*

128. HERON, *Ardea cinerea*

129. BITTERN, *Botaurus stellaris*

130. SPOONBILL, *Platalea leucorodia*

131. BEWICK'S SWAN, *Cygnus bewickii*

132. WHOOPER SWAN, *Cygnus cygnus*

133. MUTE SWAN, *Cygnus olor*

134. Greylag Goose, *Anser anser*

135. Bean Goose, *Anser fabalis*

136. PINK-FOOTED GOOSE, *Anser brachyrhynchus*

137. WHITE-FRONTED GOOSE, *Anser albifrons*

138. LESSER WHITE-FRONTED GOOSE, *Anser erythropus*

139. CANADA GOOSE, *Branta canadensis*

140. BARNACLE GOOSE, *Branta leucopsis*

141. BRENT GOOSE, *Branta bernicla*

142. SHELDUCK, *Tadorna tadorna*

143. MALLARD, *Anas platyrhynchos* ♀ ♂

144. GADWALL, *Anas strepera* ♀ ♂

145. WIGEON, *Anas penelope* ♀ ♂

146. TEAL, *Anas crecca* ♀ ♂

147. GARGANEY, *Anas querquedula* ♀ ♂

148. PINTAIL, *Anas acuta* ♂ ♀

149. SHOVELER, *Anas clypeata* ♀ ♂

150. POCHARD, *Aythya ferina* ♂ ♀

151. TUFTED DUCK, *Aythya fuligula* ♀ ♂

152. SCAUP, *Aythya marila* ♀ ♂

153. GOLDENEYE, *Bucephala clangula* ♀ ♂

154. Long-Tailed Duck, *Clangula hyemalis* ♀ ♂

155. Eider, *Somateria mollissima* ♀ ♂

156. Common Scoter, *Melanitta nigra* ♂ ♀

157. Velvet Scoter, *Melanitta fusca* ♀ ♂

158. Goosander, *Mergus merganser* ♀ above, ♂

159. Red-breasted Merganser, *Mergus serrator* ♂ ♀

160. Smew, *Mergus albellus* ♀ ♂

161. Gannet, *Sula bassana*

162. CORMORANT, *Phalacrocorax carbo*

163. SHAG, *Phalacrocorax aristotelis*

164. STORM PETREL, *Hydrobates pelagicus*

165. LEACH'S PETREL, *Oceanodroma leucorrhoa*

166. Manx Shearwater, *Puffinus puffinus*

167. Great Shearwater, *Puffinus gravis*

168. SOOTY SHEARWATER, *Puffinus griseus*

169. FULMAR, *Fulmarus glacialis*

170. GREAT CRESTED GREBE, *Podiceps cristatus*

171. RED-NECKED GREBE, *Podiceps griseigena*, winter

172. SLAVONIAN GREBE, *Podiceps auritus*

173. BLACK-NECKED GREBE, *Podiceps nigricollis*

174. LITTLE GREBE, *Tachybaptus ruficollis*

175. GREAT NORTHERN DIVER, *Gavia immer*

176. BLACK-THROATED DIVER, *Gaviá arctica*

177. RED-THROATED DIVER, *Gavia stellata*

178. WOODPIGEON, *Columba palumbus*

179. STOCK DOVE, *Columba oenas*

180. ROCK DOVE, *Columba livia*

181. TURTLE DOVE, *Streptopelia turtur*

182. BLACK-TAILED GODWIT, *Limosa limosa,* summer

183. BAR-TAILED GODWIT, *Limosa lapponica,* summer

184. CURLEW, *Numenius arquata*

185. WHIMBREL, *Numenius phaeopus*

186. WOODCOCK, *Scolopax rusticola*

187. GREAT SNIPE, *Gallinago media*

188. COMMON SNIPE, *Gallinago gallinago*

189. JACK SNIPE, *Lymnocryptes minimus*

190. GREY PHALAROPE, *Phalaropus fulicarius,* winter

191. RED-NECKED PHALAROPE, *Phalaropus lobatus,* summer

192. TURNSTONE, *Arenaria interpres*

193. KNOT, *Calidris canutus*, winter

194. DUNLIN, *Calidris alpina*

195. CURLEW SANDPIPER, *Calidris ferruginea*, winter

196. LITTLE STINT, *Calidris minuta*

197. TEMMINCK'S STINT, *Calidris temminckii*

198. Purple Sandpiper, *Calidris maritima*

199. Sanderling, *Calidris alba,* winter

200. RUFF AND REEVE, *Philomachus pugnax* ♂ ♀

201. COMMON SANDPIPER, *Tringa hypoleucos*

202. WOOD SANDPIPER, *Tringa glareola*

203. GREEN SANDPIPER, *Tringa ochropus*

204. REDSHANK, *Tringa totanus*

205. SPOTTED OR DUSKY REDSHANK
Tringa erythropus, summer

206. GREENSHANK, *Tringa nebularia*

207. KENTISH PLOVER, *Charadrius alexandrinus*

208. RINGED PLOVER, *Charadrius hiaticula*

209. LITTLE RINGED PLOVER, *Charadrius dubius*

210. GOLDEN PLOVER, *Pluvialis apricaria*

211. GREY PLOVER, *Pluvialis squatarola*, summer

212. DOTTEREL, *Eudromias morinellus*

213. LAPWING, *Vanellus vanellus*

214. BLACK-WINGED STILT, *Himantopus himantopus* ♂ ♀

215. AVOCET, *Recurvirostra avosetta*

216. OYSTERCATCHER, *Haematopus ostralegus*

217. STONE CURLEW, *Burhinus oedicnemus*

218. BLACK TERN, *Chlidonias niger*

219. GULL-BILLED TERN, *Gelochelidon nilotica*

220. SANDWICH TERN, *Sterna sandvicensis*

221. ROSEATE TERN, *Sterna dougallii*

222. COMMON TERN, *Sterna hirundo*

223. ARCTIC TERN, *Sterna paradisaea*

224. LITTLE TERN, *Sterna albifrons*

225. LITTLE GULL, *Larus minutus*, summer

226. BLACK-HEADED GULL, *Larus ridibundus,* summer

227. COMMON GULL, *Larus canus*

228. Herring Gull, *Larus argentatus*

229. Lesser Black-backed Gull, *Larus fuscus*

230. GREAT BLACK-BACKED GULL, *Larus marinus*

231. GLAUCOUS GULL, *Larus hyperboreus*

232. ICELAND GULL, *Larus glaucoides*

233. KITTIWAKE, *Rissa tridactyla*

234. GREAT SKUA, *Stercorarius skua*

235. LONG-TAILED SKUA, *Stercorarius longicaudus*

236. POMARINE SKUA, *Stercorarius pomarinus*

237. ARCTIC SKUA, *Stercorarius parasiticus*

238. RAZORBILL, *Alca torda*

239. GUILLEMOT, *Uria aalge*

240. Black Guillemot, *Cepphus grylle*

241. Little Auk, *Plautus alle*

242. PUFFIN, *Fratercula arctica*

243. CORNCRAKE, *Crex crex*

244. SPOTTED CRAKE, *Porzana porzana*

245. WATER RAIL, *Rallus aquaticus*

246. MOORHEN, *Gallinula chloropus*

247. COOT, *Fulica atra*

248. CAPERCAILLIE, *Tetrao urogallus* ♂ ♀

249. BLACK GROUSE, *Lyrurus tetrix* ♂ ♀

250. RED GROUSE, *Lagopus lagopus scoticus* ♀ ♂

251. PTARMIGAN, *Lagopus mutus* ♂ ♀

252. PHEASANT, *Phasianus colchicus* ♂

253. QUAIL, *Coturnix coturnix* on left
254. PARTRIDGE, *Perdix perdix*

255. Red-legged Partridge, *Alectoris rufa*

256. Collared Dove, *Streptopelia decaocto*

DESCRIPTIONS

PASSERINE ORDER

Most of the common land-birds and all the true song-birds.

Crow family: medium to large perching birds with glossy black or variegated plumage, usually dark legs and bills. Many of them very common in Britain. Intelligent, often omnivorous, and some highly social in their habits.

1 **Raven,** *Corvus corax*. Resident (some winter visitors) mainly in highland areas; rare east of Severn-Humber line. Frequents hilly country with crags, quarries, woods; also sea-cliffs and rocky islands. DESCRIPTION: 28 inches. Sexes alike. Biggest 'crow': long powerful bill and ruffed feathers of throat distinguish from 3. In flight shows tapered wedge-tail, wings and body more elongated than 3. VOICE: Usual call deep double croak (*cronk*). In spring, vocabulary of metallic notes, usually uttered on wing. HABITS: Walks or hops clumsily. Normal flight by slow purposeful beats or soaring, but aerobatics in spring include corkscrew dives. Forms small flocks at times and roosts socially in winter. MAY BE CONFUSED with 3.

2 **Hooded Crow,** *Corvus corone cornix*. Resident Scottish Highlands, Ireland and Man. Winter visitor to east coast, occasionally inland. DESCRIPTION: 20 inches. Sexes alike. Hybrids with 3 have black on body. VOICE: Usual note a hoarse caw, often repeated several times. HABITS: Spends much time walking or hopping on ground. Flapping flight with faster beat than 1; soaring uncommon. Flocks quite common in winter and at roosts. MAY BE CONFUSED with 3 (in silhouette) of which it is now regarded as a geographical race.

3 **Carrion Crow,** *Corvus corone corone*. Resident and winter visitor in England, Wales, southern Scotland, but increasing in Highlands where interbreeds with 2. Found generally, right into city centres. DESCRIPTION: 20 inches. Sexes alike. Tubbier than 1; in flight, wings and tail look more rounded and neck shorter. See also 4. VOICE: As 2. Many other notes recorded, including honk like old-

fashioned motor horn. HABITS: As 2. MAY BE CONFUSED with 1, 2 (in silhouette), 4.

4 **Rook,** *Corvus frugilegus.* Resident and winter visitor, but scarce in north-west Scotland. Found generally over agricultural land with small woods. DESCRIPTION: 19 inches. Sexes alike. Note purple gloss. Where 3 has tight breeches, Rook has 'plus-fours'. 3 has sloping, Rook has steep, forehead; bill looks longer and thinner. Confusion most likely between 3 and young Rooks which have no white patch on face. VOICE: Typical caw less hoarse than 2 and 3. Many notes heard at rookeries and roosts. HABITS: Feeds mainly on ground, walking about slowly. Rather fast flapping flight and soaring evolutions common. Social throughout life. Accompanied in many districts by 5. MAY BE CONFUSED with 3, 5.

5 **Jackdaw,** *Corvus monedula.* Resident, some summer and winter visitors; scarce in north-west Scotland. Found over agricultural land and suburbia; also neighbourhood of crags and quarries, including sea-cliffs. DESCRIPTION: 14 inches. Sexes alike. Eye has prominent light iris. Usually seen with 4, when smaller size and more erect stance are obvious. VOICE: Single *jack* note often develops into chuckle or cackle, quite distinct from caw of 4 when they are flying together. Calls of juveniles can be confused with those of 8. HABITS: Quick walking action on ground, but spends much time aloft. Flapping flight with quicker beats than 4; soaring and aerobatics in flocks. Though extremely social, pairs can often be distinguished as flocks wheel in air. MAY BE CONFUSED with 4, 8.

6 **Magpie,** *Pica pica.* Resident; general England, Wales, Ireland, Man, but local or absent in Scotland. Frequents agricultural land and suburbia; not in large woods. DESCRIPTION: 19 inches (half of it tail). Sexes alike. Distinctive pied appearance. VOICE: Angry chattering call most commonly heard. More musical notes in spring. HABITS: Feeds much on ground, walking or hopping when excited. Perches high in trees showing unmistakable, long-tailed silhouette, also obvious in rather slow flapping flight. MAY BE CONFUSED with 54.

7 **Jay,** *Garrulus glandarius.* Resident; general England and Wales; widespread in Ireland (distinct race); local in Scotland. Wooded country, especially oakwoods. DESCRIPTION: 14 inches. Sexes alike. Eye blue. White rump and blue on wing are features which

identify. VOICE: Shrieking alarm calls and cat-like mewing reveal usually hidden Jays. HABITS: Skulking; sometimes on ground where it hops. Usually seen in heavy flapping flight between thick cover, but sometimes visits gardens to eat peas, etc. MAY BE CONFUSED with 98.

8 **Chough,** *Pyrrhocorax pyrrhocorax.* Resident; now extinct Cornwall; local western Welsh coast and inland in North Wales; Isle of Man; S.Inner Hebrides; quite common parts of Irish coast. Sea-cliffs, quarries, old mines; occasionally inland crags. DESCRIPTION: 15 inches, including long bill. Sexes alike. Extended feathers when soaring distinguish from 5. VOICE: Resembles 5, but sounds more musical and two syllables more distinct. Confusion possible with juvenile 5. HABITS: Runs or hops on ground. Flicks tail and wings when calling. Seen much in air soaring like miniature eagle rather than crow, but in flapping flight may be confused with 5. Often in parties up to 50, but pairs may nest alone. MAY BE CONFUSED with 5.

Starling family: only one common species.

9 **Starling,** *Sturnus vulgaris.* Resident and winter visitor. General, except parts of western Ireland. Towns, villages, and farms but also sea cliffs in Scotland and Ireland. DESCRIPTION: 8½ inches. Sexes much alike, but female more spotted. Summer male is shown; at other times has varying amount of pale spots. Both sexes much browner on back in winter. Bill dark in winter. Juveniles at first almost uniform brown but in autumn show brown heads and glossy bodies. VOICE: Churring alarm, whistle, and cat-call are common notes. Song imitates many other birds expertly. HABITS: All movements fast and bustling; runs rapidly on ground where most feeding takes place. Fast whirring flight with stout body and short tail. Social at all times, building up into enormous roosts. MAY BE CONFUSED with small waders when feeding on shore or marsh. Juveniles often mistaken for rarities, e.g. Rose-coloured Starling.

Oriole family: only one rare species.

10 **Golden Oriole,** *Oriolus oriolus.* Regular visitor on migration; has nested. Mostly recorded in southern England in thick woodland, especially oak. DESCRIPTION: 9½ inches. Male as shown,

female a duller yellow-green, pale and streaked underneath, wings and tail dark brownish. VOICE: Beautiful two or three note whistle of male suggested by German name *Pirol*. Also screeches and cat-calls like 7. HABITS: Very difficult to see; spends most time in thick cover. Fast but heavy and undulating flight with final sweep up to perch. Usually in ones or twos in Britain. MAY BE CONFUSED with 78, 101.

Finch family: small to small-medium perching birds, often with forked tails and all with stout, seed-eating bills. Sexes usually differ. Characteristic flight, dipping when wings close. Musical rather metallic call-notes. Most species form winter flocks, often mixing with other finches. Family includes **buntings,** streaky brown birds usually with prominent white outer tail-feathers.

11 **Hawfinch,** *Coccothraustes coccothraustes.* Resident, local in England, Wales, and southern Scotland. Thick woodland, large gardens and orchards. DESCRIPTION: 7 inches. Sexes much alike. Stout, short-tailed big-headed finch with massive bill. In flight white wing bar and tail border show up. Female paler and duller generally. Juvenile shows barring and has no black bib. VOICE: Usually recognized by *chip* call, rather like that of 102. HABITS: Elusive and skulking, especially in breeding season. Sometimes appears on tree-tops and on fruiting bushes when extracting seeds. Seldom on ground, where it hops, but can be attracted to water. MAY BE CONFUSED with 12, 20.

12 **Greenfinch,** *Carduelis chloris.* Resident and winter visitor; general on British and Irish mainland. Gardens, hedgerows, woodland edge; farmyards in winter. DESCRIPTION: 6 inches. Sexes much alike. Stocky, thick-billed finch with short forked tail. Yellow patches show up in flight. Female duller than male, with some streaking. Juvenile, quite brown, often mistaken for rare relatives, but has yellow on wings and tail. VOICE: Short *chip* call often repeated rapidly many times; also a much more musical call of two syllables. Male's *jee* call in spring and summer distinctive; also warbling song, often uttered in flight. HABITS: Often perches prominently on bushes and trees and feeds on ground where it hops. Male's slow flapping butterfly flight catches eye in spring. Flocks in winter, often with other finches. MAY BE CONFUSED with 11, 14, 20 (female).

13 **Goldfinch,** *Carduelis carduelis*. Resident and summer visitor, now fairly general except northern Scotland. Gardens, orchards, hedgerows, avenues; riverside alders and waste ground in winter. DESCRIPTION: 5 inches. Sexes alike. Adult plumage unique. Juvenile is streaky and has no head pattern, but wing as adult. VOICE: Musical call note defies description but once associated with bird is diagnostic; also a loud double alarm note. Musical-box song recalls canary. HABITS: Typically flits about in parties, perching on thistles and other seed-heads; sometimes on ground where it hops. Flocks in autumn and for roosting.

14 **Siskin,** *Carduelis spinus*. Resident and widespread winter visitor; now breeds commonly parts of Scotland (especially Highlands) and Ireland, locally in N. Wales and England south to Devon in open conifer areas, including large gardens; in winter typically in riverside alders. DESCRIPTION: 5 inches. Sexes differ. Rump yellow; dark and light bars on wing. Juvenile like female but browner. Much smaller than 12, and no bright yellow on wings and tail. VOICE: Loud, questioning *pchee?* often drawn out and used on wing; also twitters on wing. Song a canary-like medley ending in a long note. HABITS: Party usually seen as cluster on alders, flying away in an undulating ball to a fresh tree; but also low on thistles etc. Song flights and chases in breeding areas. Occasionally solitary. MAY BE CONFUSED with 12, 15 (in silhouette).

15 **Redpoll,** *Acanthis flammea*. Resident, summer and winter visitor; local in southern England, becoming much commoner in north, west, and in Wales, Scotland, and Ireland. In winter much as 14. A distinguishable race, the Mealy Redpoll, occurs in small numbers. Breeds in low scrub: thorns, birch and sallow. In winter amongst alders and birches. DESCRIPTION: 5 inches. Sexes rather alike. Female and juveniles (not shown) lack pink breast. Mealy Redpoll has cleaner, brighter plumage and shows two pale bars on wing. VOICE: Repeated chittering call *shee shee shee shee* ... uttered in flight. Song much poorer than those of relatives. HABITS: Behaviour much as 14, but call notes quite distinct. Song flights in spring. MAY BE CONFUSED with 14 (in silhouette), 17 (in flight).

16 **Twite,** *Acanthis flavirostris*. Resident; breeds northern England and Scottish Highlands, coastal counties of Ireland, and many islands. Moorland and coastal strips, including cultivated

areas. Southern coastal areas and moors in winter. DESCRIPTION: 5 inches. Sexes rather alike and resemble female or juvenile 17. In winter yellow bill distinguishes and male always has pinkish rump. Distinguished from 15 by absence of head markings. VOICE: Sharp, twanging call note best distinguishing feature. Song like 17, but also more twanging. HABITS: Much on ground where it hops, but also perches freely, e.g. on roadside fence wires. Often breeds in groups and flocks in autumn, roosting socially. MAY BE CONFUSED with 15, 17.

17 Linnet, *Acanthis cannabina.* Resident, summer and winter visitor; general except northern Scotland. Gorse heaths, hedgerows and gardens, coastal dunes and links. In winter often in stubbles. DESCRIPTION: 5 inches. Sexes differ somewhat. Male shown in spring; loses colour in winter but chestnut back distinguishes from streaky brown female and juvenile (and from 15 and 16). VOICE: Repeated call note on wing, less metallic than 15 and 16, is best guide. Pretty rippling song recalls canary. HABITS: Feeds mainly on ground where it hops. Often breeds in groups and large flocks form in autumn and for roosting. MAY BE CONFUSED with 15, 16.

18 **Bullfinch,** *Pyrrhula pyrrhula.* Resident, some winter visitors of northern race. General except northern Scotland, where local. Thickets rather than tall woods; gardens and orchards. DESCRIPTION: 6 inches. Sexes differ. Juvenile much as female without black cap. VOICE: Single, double, or triple plaintive *pew, pew-her, pew-her-her.* No true song. HABITS: Very rarely on ground where it hops; pairs or small parties travel through bushes calling, then settle to attack buds, fruit, or seeds. Dipping finch flight when stubby head shows in silhouette.

19 **Scarlet Rosefinch,** *Carpodacus erythrinus.* Rare visitor, mainly east coast and Shetland. DESCRIPTION: 6 inches. Sexes differ. When seen in Britain birds are in brown autumn plumage, rather like female 30 but with two pale wing-bars; throat is streaked. Male as shown resembles 20 but without crossed mandibles. VOICE: Double canary-like call-note. HABITS: Short-necked posture said to be characteristic, like small 23. British visitors occur in open, treeless country where they perch on fence-wires. MAY BE CONFUSED with (in Britain) 20 (male, in summer), 23, 30 (female).

20 **Crossbill,** *Loxia curvirostra.* Scottish race, considered by some authorities to be race of Parrot Crossbill, *L. pytyopsittacus,* is resident, confined to central Highlands; typical race 'irrupts', then becomes resident, breeding locally East Anglia, Hampshire, perhaps Surrey; has bred in many English and Irish counties. Found in open fir woods, especially Scots pines. DESCRIPTION: 6½ inches. Sexes differ. Young males orange-yellow; juvenile grey-green and heavily streaked, lacking cross-bill may be mistaken for 12 but has no bright yellow. Absence of white wing-bar distinguishes all plumages from 11. VOICE: Ringing *chip chip* call, often repeated several times, is louder than similar calls of 12 and 31 and identifies flying parties. Querulous call from perch *tukay, tukayo* lengthens into usual song. HABITS: Allows close approach when feeding on trees (cones) or fruiting bushes; only abnormally on ground or when drinking. Parties when feeding resemble small parrots. Song flights in spring. Social at all times. MAY BE CONFUSED with 11, 12, 19.

21 **Chaffinch,** *Fringilla coelebs.* Resident and winter visitor; in bush and tree cover of all kinds. DESCRIPTION: 6 inches. Sexes differ. Bright and varied colours of male should be unmistakable. Juveniles resemble female. VOICE: Ringing *pink* call when perched and staccato *sip* in flight; many others recorded. Simple song: *chit chit chit chit chee cha* has many variants. HABITS: Often on ground where it hops or runs. Likes prominent song perches. Flocks in autumn and often mixes with other species and for roosting. MAY BE CONFUSED with 22, 58 (females).

22 **Brambling,** *Fringilla montifringilla.* Winter visitor; has bred. Fairly general, but much scarcer in west and north-west. In beechwoods till beechmast exhausted, then farmland. DESCRIPTION: 6 inches. Sexes differ. Winter male lacks blue head of spring (as shown). Female (not shown) like female 21, but with black streaks on head, orange breast, white rump and forked tail as male. VOICE: Call-note when perched a rather harsh *scape* quite unlike 21; flight call hoarser than 21. HABITS: Forms flocks, sometimes with 21, feeding on ground where it hops and runs, and flying up to perch when disturbed, thus showing white rump. MAY BE CONFUSED with 21.

23 **Corn Bunting,** *Emberiza calandra.* Resident; locally common on east side Britain, but absent or very local in west and Ireland and

more or less confined to coast. Open agricultural or marginal land right to coast. DESCRIPTION: 7 inches. Sexes alike. A squat rather short-tailed brown bird lacking any distinguishing mark. Absence of crest and of white outer tail-feathers separate it from 33; much bigger than female 30. VOICE: Call-note an abrupt *tsip*, sometimes broken into several syllables. Song, traditionally described as jangling of small silver keys, quite distinctive. HABITS: Males on song perches (bushes, posts, telegraph wires) are typical of breeding areas. Difficult to see on ground, where feeding takes place at slow walk. Flight heavy and fluttering but rather like 33. Small flocks form after breeding season and roost socially. MAY BE CONFUSED with 19, 30 (female), 33.

24 **Ortolan,** *Emberiza hortulana.* Rare visitor, chiefly along south and east coasts north to Shetland in autumn, but some in spring. DESCRIPTION: 6 inches. Sexes rather alike. Green head of male (as shown) should be distinctive; female is rather duller. Juveniles lack head-dress but all show narrow ring round eye and rather pinkish underparts. VOICE: Variety of short calls. HABITS: Likely to be seen on ground, where it runs, or perching on wires. MAY BE CONFUSED with 25, 26 (adults).

25 **Yellowhammer,** *Emberiza citrinella.* Resident and winter visitor; mainly agricultural land with hedgerows but also heathery country. DESCRIPTION: 6½ inches. Sexes rather alike. Typical male (as shown) but some females have practically no yellow and are streaky brown birds with white outer tail-feathers. Much variation and some females brighter than some males. Both have rufous rumps, very obvious in flight. VOICE: Several call-notes based on ringing *trit*. Song traditional *little bit of bread and no cheese.* HABITS: Singing males perch high along summer hedgerows. Feeds on ground, hopping and running. Flight less dipping than true finches and sometimes quite straight. Flocks in autumn and winter, often with 12 and 21. MAY BE CONFUSED with 24, 26, 30 (females).

26 **Cirl Bunting,** *Emberiza cirlus.* Resident, local in southern and south-western England, as far as Malvern; but not now in North Wales. Wooded fringes of chalk downs and other hillsides, often near sea. DESCRIPTION: 6 inches. Sexes differ. Female very like dark female 25, but both sexes distinguished from 25 by olive-brown rump. VOICE: *Zip* call quite unlike

any note of 25. Song a rattle, rather like beginning of 25 song but even more like 76. HABITS: Perches higher than other buntings, often in hedgerow elms. Feeds on ground e.g. in farmyards, where it walks and hops. Dipping finch-like flight. MAY BE CONFUSED with 24, 25, 30 (females).

27 **Reed Bunting,** *Emberiza schoeniclus*. Resident, summer and winter visitor on all types of marshy or drier ground with thick vegetation; in winter often in agricultural land. DESCRIPTION: 6 inches. Sexes differ. In winter male's head becomes much duller. Females and young males have strongly streaked brown head markings. Both sexes have prominent white outer tail-feathers. VOICE: Calls a drawn-out *zeep* and a shorter metallic note. Song a simple *chee chee chee chihitty*, with varying emphasis. HABITS: Usually seen clinging to a reed or similar plant. Seldom visible on ground and reluctant to fly far, but makes short bobbing flights from perch to perch. MAY BE CONFUSED with 28, 30 (females).

28 **Lapland Bunting,** *Calcarius lapponicus*. Passage migrant (mainly autumn) and rare winter visitor, chiefly to eastern coastal counties. DESCRIPTION: 6 inches. Sexes differ. Male's head-dress much duller in autumn. Female rather sparrow-like brown bird and young male resembles her with pale underparts. White outer feathers of rather short tail not very conspicuous. Yellow bill is useful feature. VOICE: Usual autumn note a toneless *tuctuctuc*, like call of 23 repeated, and often followed by a musical whistle. HABITS: Feeds on shore or coastal fields where it runs freely but can hop. Usually in small parties which roost on ground and may associate with larks and other buntings. MAY BE CONFUSED with 27.

29 **Snow Bunting,** *Plectrophenax nivalis*. Winter visitor; a few pairs breed on high Scottish hills, otherwise in winter along east coast and in some moorland and mountainous areas. DESCRIPTION: 6½ inches. Sexes differ. In winter (not shown) both sexes warm brown above with white underparts, but show varying amounts of white on wings and tail in flight. In summer male (as shown) is unmistakable, but female retains brown, streaked with black on head and back. Bill yellow with dark tip in winter. VOICE: Usual call in winter an attractive twitter with emphasis at the end. HABITS: Habitually on ground, running about to feed, but

flock moves by last birds flying up to settle in front. Rather fast dipping flight. Normally in flocks in Britain in winter. MAY BE CONFUSED (female) with 33.

Sparrow family: Finch-like little birds which live socially; only two common species.

30 **House Sparrow,** *Passer domesticus.* Resident; always in association with man; towns, villages, farms; in farmland in autumn. DESCRIPTION: 6 inches. Sexes differ. Juveniles at first like female. VOICE: Variety of notes in which *jick jick jiddick* is prominent but has variations. Best effort at song is series of chirps. HABITS: Lively hops characteristic. Lives socially and flocks fly up with noisy whirring. Periodical bedlams called 'sparrows' weddings' are form of courtship. Roosts socially but sometimes scattered. MAY BE CONFUSED (male) with 31; female with several buntings and with 90.

31 **Tree Sparrow,** *Passer montanus.* Resident (some winter visitors and passage migrants); locally common England, Wales, south Scotland; local but increasing north Scotland and Ireland. Agricultural land with old trees, orchards, or buildings for nesting. DESCRIPTION: 5½ inches. Sexes alike. A smaller, cleaner-looking edition of male 30. Crown all bright chestnut, black crescent on white cheeks; two narrow wing-bars. VOICE: *Chip* note resembles but is more refined than chirp of 30; also a finch-like flight note *chick chick*. Song a chirping prattle superior to 30. HABITS: Seldom on ground; perches on trees and buildings and is often hard to see. Nests socially and flocks in autumn, associating with finches and buntings rather than 30. Flight finch-like, less noisy than 30. MAY BE CONFUSED with 30 (male).

Lark family: small to small-medium brown birds with fairly stout bills, living in open country. Sexes usually alike. Running gait, dipping flight like finches.

32 **Woodlark,** *Lullula arborea.* Resident, southern half of England and Wales, but very local. Open short grassland with bushes, e.g. downs, brecks, and heaths. DESCRIPTION: 6 inches. Sexes alike. Noticeably short tail. Stripes over eyes meet behind and

distinguish from 33; also little black and white 'flash' at elbow of wing. Plumage generally more mottled than 33 and lacks prominent white outer tail-feathers. VOICE: Call-note a musical *titlooet* and beautiful song develops from this, a limpid repeated *lou* being one of its features. HABITS: Usually seen on ground, where it runs, but perches on trees and wires; sings mostly on wing in wide circles. Normal flight clumsy and heavy with exaggerated dips. MAY BE CONFUSED with 33.

33 **Skylark**, *Alauda arvensis*. Resident (summer and winter visitor, passage migrant) in all kinds of open country, except wet moorland. DESCRIPTION: 7 inches. Sexes alike. Bigger, better proportioned than 32. Longer tail has prominent white outer feathers but crest less pronounced. Juveniles appear yellower, and their shorter tails may cause confusion with 32. VOICE: Call a two-syllable chirp, a little like that of 25. Song continuous and unmistakable. HABITS: Usually on ground, standing up or crouching and running; but often perches on posts and bushes. Song uttered in flight; occasionally from perch. Rapid fluttering flight when put up and rising to sing, also sustained dipping action. Roosts on ground. Flocks in autumn and winter. MAY BE CONFUSED with 23, 29, 32.

34 **Shorelark**, *Eremophila alpestris*. Rare winter visitor to English east coast; on shingle shores with weed patches. DESCRIPTION: 6½ inches. Sexes rather alike. Male has more black on breast and little black horns in spring. VOICE: Variety of notes resembling those of pipits and wagtails; a musical *seep* the most distinctive. HABITS: Almost exclusively on ground, where it runs or hops. In Britain small parties, often associating with other larks and buntings, are quite easy to approach. Dipping flight.

Pipit and Wagtail family: small birds of open country usually with prominent white outer tail-feathers, running gait, and dipping flight. Insect-eaters. **Pipits** are streaky brown, like small, longer-legged larks with sexes similar. **Wagtails** have variegated plumage, long tails and sexes differ somewhat; usually found near water.

35 **Tawny Pipit**, *Anthus campestris*. Rare visitor on passage mainly to coast of south-east England. DESCRIPTION: 6½ inches. Sexes alike. A big, sandy-brown pipit, showing light stripe over eye and pale underparts. Juveniles more streaked. VOICE:

Call-note a variable *seep*. MAY BE CONFUSED with other pipits and 41.

36 Tree Pipit, *Anthus trivialis.* Summer visitor (mid-April); general in Britain except extreme north; absent Ireland and Man. Rather varied habitats from open woodland to heaths, bracken slopes and marshes with scattered trees as perches. DESCRIPTION: 6 inches. Sexes alike. Resembles 37, but less olive, a little bigger and more upstanding. VOICE: Call-note a long *seep*. Bubbling cadence of song uttered usually in paper dart flight downwards from perch identifies. HABITS: Feeds on ground, walking, and stopping to elongate neck and peer round. Ordinary flight dipping and rather irregular. MAY BE CONFUSED with other pipits, especially 37.

37 Meadow Pipit, *Anthus pratensis.* Resident (summer and winter visitor, passage migrant) on moorlands, rough pastures, heaths, downs, and coastal dunes. DESCRIPTION: 6 inches. Sexes alike. Very like 36, but generally more olive-brown and slightly smaller. VOICE: Shrill *pipit* call, often repeated several times, quite distinct from call of 36. Song cadence, though similar, is inferior and uttered differently, male flying up and gliding down without using a perch. HABITS: Essentially a ground bird, though will perch freely on posts, bushes, and rocks. Perhaps more active than 36 but hard to tell from 38 when they overlap. Birds fly up calling as intruder crosses breeding area. Flocks and parties form in autumn. MAY BE CONFUSED with 36, 38.

38 Rock Pipit, *Anthus spinoletta.* Resident (some winter visitors) on rocky coasts and islands. DESCRIPTION: 6 inches. Sexes alike. Rather bigger than 36 and 37. Outer tail-feathers light grey, not white. Legs dark brown (a useful point). VOICE: *Pipit* call hard to tell from that of 37 but not so shrill. Loud insistent *chip* of alarm. Song between that of 36 and 37 in quality, delivered like 37. HABITS: A coastal bird, feeding on or below tide-line, often in line of wrack. Rather wavering flight, showing outer tail-feathers. When with young, perches on rock and scolds intruder monotonously. MAY BE CONFUSED with 36, 37.

39 Grey Wagtail, *Motacilla cinerea.* Resident, local in south-east, general elsewhere. By rocky, fast-flowing waters or by weirs etc. on slow-flowing waters. In winter round farms and even in towns. DESCRIPTION: 7 inches (including tail). Sexes differ slightly. Male as shown; female has white throat and male in winter resembles her. Juvenile has pinkish breast and shorter tail. VOICE: Repeated call-note rather like that of 43: *tsip-tsip-tsip*, sometimes only single *tsi-ip*. Song four repeated call-notes, followed by four 'echoing' notes. HABITS: Typically seen dipping and flirting tail on boulder in stream. Runs quickly when feeding on ground; catches flies on wing. Flies with very pronounced dips, calling. MAY BE CONFUSED with 40, 41.

40 Blue-headed Wagtail, *Motacilla flava flava.* Continental race of 41; passage migrant, mainly along east coast and in south-east England; has bred. Marshy fields, bulb farms, and arable land. DESCRIPTION: 6½ inches (including tail). Sexes differ. Male in spring as shown. Female browner, lacks head pattern, but has stripe over eye. Winter male resembles female. VOICE: Call-note a penetrating *tseep*, cut off at end. Short warbling song not often heard. HABITS: Habitually on ground, often amongst cattle, running quickly and snapping at insects. Dipping flight less pronounced than 39. Different habitat, shorter tail, and absence of black throat should distinguish from male 39. In parties on migration, but usually with 41. MAY BE CONFUSED with 39, 41. Several other races of 'Yellow' Wagtails have occurred in Britain; the male of one is also shown in the picture; it comes from south-east Europe.

41 Yellow Wagtail, *Motacilla flava flavissima.* British race of 40. Summer visitor (mid-April) and passage migrant. Widespread and locally common in England and Wales; very local southern Scotland and only irregular Ireland. Marshy fields, heaths, and upland pastures in north, arable land, coastal dunes. DESCRIPTION: 6½ inches. Sexes differ. Female as female 40 but with less pronounced stripe over eye. Both much sandier than any plumage of 39. VOICE and HABITS: as 40. MAY BE CONFUSED with 35, 39 (often called the Yellow Wagtail in districts where this species does not occur), 40.

42 White Wagtail, *Motacilla alba alba.* European race of 43. Passage migrant mainly along coasts but often recorded inland; has bred. Riverside and coastal fields and dunes; ploughed fields inland. DESCRIPTION: 7 inches (including tail). Sexes almost alike. Adults in spring have clear grey back and rump which distinguishes them from 43. In autumn females and juveniles have white throats and all upper-parts, including head, grey, and are duller than males; juveniles also lack the black breast and have general brownish tinge. VOICE: Usual call-note rather piercing *chizzick* or *zick*, distinguishable from 39. Song, not often heard, a pleasant chattering warble embodying the call-notes. HABITS: Runs about quickly, feeding on ground; also perches freely on posts, buildings, and sometimes trees. In parties on migration. MAY BE CONFUSED with 43.

43 **Pied Wagtail,** *Motacilla alba yarrellii.* British race of 42. Resident and summer visitor, usually in neighbourhood of running water, and of big houses, ruins, and roadsides with stone walls. DESCRIPTION: 7 inches. Sexes differ somewhat. Spring male like 42, but black replaces grey everywhere except flanks; female has upper back dark grey, but rump black. In winter throat is white in both and female is greyer on head and breast. Juveniles are browny-grey but have some white on forehead and black on crown distinguishing them from 42. VOICE: as 42 but notes perhaps harsher. HABITS: as 42, but large communal roosts in reed-beds, bushes, trees in towns even in greenhouses and factories. MAY BE CONFUSED with 42.

Tit family and 'allies': small or very small, very active arboreal (except 53) birds, hanging dexterously under twigs etc. and making short, round-winged flights. **Tits** are bright-plumaged, sexes more or less alike and primarily insect-eaters; their 'allies', Nuthatch and Treecreeper, are specialized tree-trunk climbers. All form mixed flocks in winter.

44 **Nuthatch,** *Sitta europea.* Resident in most of Southern England and Wales, becoming local or absent in north; not Scotland or Ireland. Woodland (especially oak and beech, not conifers), large gardens, and parks. DESCRIPTION: 5½ inches. Sexes alike. Unique in appearance. Rounded wings black, outer tail-feathers black with white spots which show in flight. VOICE: A variety of calls, of which series of ringing *plinks* is most readily recognized; also a tit-like *tsit.* Songs include a repeated, drawn-out *twee* and a series of shorter notes which are very like similar cries of 103, 104, and 112. HABITS: Arboreal, but occasionally feeds on ground where it hops. Runs up and down trees in short bursts, stopping to hold head away from trunk. Long flights dipping; also whirrs from tree to tree. Wedges nuts, etc., in cracks and

hammers them noisily. Roosts in holes. Often with flocks of tits in winter.

45 **Treecreeper**, *Certhia familiaris*. Resident in woods of all types, gardens, and hedgerows with old trees. DESCRIPTION: 5 inches. Sexes alike. A slender mouse-like bird with stiff, rufous fantail; rounded wings show pale band in flight. VOICE: Call a thin but penetrating *zee zee zee*, easy to confuse at first with some tit calls. Song begins *zee zee zee* and ends in scurry of notes. HABITS: Runs up trees, keeping close to trunk and using tail as prop, then flutters down to start again; seldom makes long flights. Probes bark with bill. Roosts in cavities. Associates with tits. NOTE: This species is replaced in Channel Islands by very similar **Short-toed Treecreeper** *Certhia brachydactyla*, which has recently been identified in southern England, breeding in 1971.

46 **Great Tit**, *Parus major*. Resident in woodlands, gardens, wooded farmland. DESCRIPTION: $5\frac{1}{2}$ inches. Sexes differ somewhat. The largest tit, with black band, much wider in male and expanding over belly, dividing yellow breast. Note also white wing-bar and white outer tail feathers. VOICE: A great variety of calls: a hollow *pink* like Chaffinch, a repeated *tewi*, a scolding *i-chi chi chi . . .* etc. Song, a repeated *teacher teacher* with emphasis on second syllable, described, according to taste, as like a saw sharpening or a fairy bell ringing! HABITS: Mainly arboreal, but feeds occasionally on ground where it hops. Joins up in parties with other tits and small birds in autumn. Roosts in cavities. MAY BE CONFUSED with 48, 50, 51.

47 **Blue Tit**, *Parus caeruleus*. Resident in woodlands, gardens, wooded farmland, further into towns than 46. DESCRIPTION: $4\frac{1}{2}$ inches. Sexes very alike. A small tit with general blue effect of upperparts. Juveniles have white areas washed yellow. VOICE: A variety of calls of which buzzing *zee zee zee zit* is characteristic. Explosive scolding note. *Zee* notes introduce song rather like that of 45 in form but more forceful and musical. HABITS: Very like small 46, but, on the whole, feeds higher in foliage and lands on ground less often; perhaps the most acrobatic of the tits. Habit of raising back feathers of crown has caused confusion with 49 in bad light.

48 **Coal Tit**, *Parus ater*. Resident in woodland with preference for

conifers or highland oakwoods. DESCRIPTION: 4 inches. Sexes alike. A very small tit with relatively big head, dull black but with white cheeks and broad white stripe up nape to crown. VOICE: Call-notes a rather thin but musical *tswee* and a shriller *tsee* very like note of 60. Songs either repeated *teacher* as 46, with emphasis on first or second syllable, or a scurrying phrase resembling song of 45. HABITS: in general much as other tits, but often more difficult to see when high in conifers. MAY BE CONFUSED with 46, 50, 51, 60 (by voice or in silhouette).

49 **Crested Tit,** *Parus cristatus*. Resident, confined to pine woods of eastern Scottish Highlands. DESCRIPTION: 4½ inches. Sexes alike as shown. VOICE: Distinctive call-note, which may be song when repeated; can be roughly represented as *prrrrrr;* also a shrill triple *zee*. HABITS: in general as other tits; said to feed a good deal on tree trunks. MAY BE CONFUSED with 47 (in bad light).

50 **Marsh Tit,** *Parus palustris*. Resident, general to local in England and Wales, just reaching south-east Scotland; absent Ireland. Woodland, gardens, and wooded farmland. DESCRIPTION: 4 inches. Sexes alike. A small black-headed tit with glossy crown, greyish cheeks, and neat black bib. Impossible to tell from 51 on plumage with absolute certainty, though appears a more alert and tidier bird. VOICE: Two calls: *pitchu* and *tchickabeebe* distinct from any call of 51; also *tcha* much less sustained than similar note of 51. Song a repeated *tschuppi* or variants on this and on the *pitchu* call. HABITS: Much as other tits, but feeds on lower growth, especially on tall thistles in late summer. MAY BE CONFUSED with 46, 48, 51 (especially), 74.

51 **Willow Tit,** *Parus montanus*. Resident, locally common England and Wales; very local south Scotland, absent Ireland. Scrub-woods, especially alder, birch, and elder clumps. DESCRIPTION: 4 inches. Sexes alike. Plumage as 50, but crown dull, smoky black, often a pale patch on wings when folded and black bib more extensive. General appearance curiously unkempt as compared with dapper 50. VOICE: Call-note a harsh squeezed-out *tchay*, often repeated three times and quite distinguishable; also a quiet *zit zit* which 50 does not have, and which may introduce the *tchay* note. Usual song a repeated *piu* like song of 64. HABITS: Feeds lower down than most tits and at times plunges deep into cover like a Wren. Rather more solitary than relatives

but sometimes in mixed parties. MAY BE CONFUSED with 50.

52 **Long-tailed Tit,** *Aegithalos caudatus.* Resident in woodland and woodland edge, especially blackthorn thickets and hedgerows. DESCRIPTION: 5½ inches (tail 3). Sexes alike. Unique in appearance: very small mouse-like bird with very short bill and very long tail. White on wings and on outer feathers of black tail shows in flight. Juveniles darker and less pink. VOICE: Call-notes a repeated insistent *zitzitzit* and a single staccato *zip,* sometimes extended and trilled. HABITS: Almost exclusively arboreal, parties travelling rapidly through trees or bushes. Flight silhouette unmistakable as tiny bodies and long tails dip and bob across open spaces. Roosts in parties jammed close together.

53 **Bearded Tit or Reedling,** *Panurus biarmicus.* Resident in reed-beds of east and south-east England, whence may erupt in autumn as far west as Wales. DESCRIPTION: 6½ inches (tail 3). Sexes differ, as shown. Juveniles as female, though young male has small black moustache. Bill of male a striking yellow, bill of female much duller; eye noticeably light. VOICE: Distinctive call a loud *ping ping tic* emerging from conversational notes of parties. HABITS: Lives exclusively in reed-beds, parties appearing occasionally to whirr like miniature Pheasants over their tops. Note: The Bearded Tit is now regarded as the only European member of the Babbler family.

Shrike family: Medium to small-medium perching birds, resembling birds of prey in habits. Striking plumage and habit of perching on tops of bushes whence they make hawking flights.

54 **Great Grey Shrike,** *Lanius excubitor.* Rare winter visitor and passage migrant, occurring mostly on east side of Britain in open country with scattered thorn bushes. DESCRIPTION: 9½ inches. Sexes almost alike. Underparts white with faint wavy markings in female and juvenile. VOICE: Generally silent in Britain but has a harsh Magpie-like chatter. HABITS: Round-winged flight rather like 6. Solitary, may return to same winter haunt several years running. MAY BE CONFUSED in outline with 6, and with very rare Lesser Grey Shrike (not shown).

55 **Red-backed Shrike,** *Lanius collurio.* Summer visitor (early May), now confined to south and east of Wash-Bristol Channel line and still decreasing. Gorse-clad heaths, scrub-land with thorn

and briar bushes; old hedges. DESCRIPTION: 7 inches. Sexes differ. Male, as shown; female lacks head-pattern, has brown tail and wavy brown bars over underparts. Juvenile similar and very difficult to tell from juveniles of some rare shrikes. VOICE: Most commonly heard note is harsh, clacking alarm call. Song, seldom heard, is surprisingly sweet warble, which rambles on, sometimes mimicking other birds. HABITS: Quickly recognized by prominent perching. Broad-winged swooping flight like small 7. Hawks for insects, and makes larders of its kills. MAY BE CONFUSED (female) with 72, 79.

Waxwing family: only one species in Britain.

56 **Waxwing,** *Bombycilla garrulus.* Irregular winter visitor, mainly to east coast, but in some years spreads to west. Usually seen in neighbourhood of berry-bearing bushes. DESCRIPTION: 7 inches. Sexes alike. In shape rather like 9, but with obvious crest. Juveniles duller, with no bibs at first. VOICE: Usually silent in Britain, but has rather weak *tsirr* call. HABITS: Flocks, small parties and single birds haunt berry-bearing bushes, showing indifference to man and often appearing in gardens and busy towns. Strong flight with long, shallow dips as wings close. MAY BE CONFUSED (in distance only) with parties of 9, 79, 80.

Flycatcher family: small summer visitors, arboreal and catching much of their insect food by aerial sallies. Sexes sometimes distinct.

57 **Spotted Flycatcher,** *Muscicapa striata.* Summer visitor (first half May), near habitations of all kinds well into suburbia; also woodland edge. DESCRIPTION: 5½ inches. Sexes alike. Slim, upright bird with rather abrupt forehead. Darker wings show in flight. Only juveniles are spotted. VOICE: Usual call-note shrill *tzee* becoming explosive *tzee-tuck*. Squeaky little song can be heard soon after arrival. HABITS: Perches prominently, making sallies into air after flies and returning to same perch, where flicks rather long tail. Flight moth-like when pursuing prey; sustained flight seldom seen. MAY BE CONFUSED with 58 (female) and (at a distance) with several warblers.

58 **Pied Flycatcher,** *Ficedula hypoleuca.* Summer visitor (mid-April) and passage migrant, local western, northern England and

southern Scotland; locally common Wales; rare Scottish High-lands; on passage elsewhere. Woodland (oak, birch, alder), parks, and gardens in highland areas. DESCRIPTION: 5 inches. Sexes differ. Male in autumn (and occasionally in breeding season) resembles brown female. Juvenile scaly like 57 but shows yellowy-white wing-bar. VOICE: Usual call-note a repeated *tic*, becoming a fierce staccato *tacc* of alarm. Common version of variable song may be rendered *tchee tchee tchee tchay-char*. HABITS: Perches on dead snags etc. below canopy of woodland, making sallies but not usually returning to same perch. Often lands on ground and hops. Fluttering flight shows white wing-bars. MAY BE CONFUSED (female) with 21 (female), 57; (male) with 94.

59 **Red-breasted Flycatcher,** *Ficedula parva*. Rare passage migrant, mainly east coast and Shetland. DESCRIPTION: 4½ inches. Sexes differ. A small flycatcher, characterized in all plumages by white patches on black tail. VOICE: Call-note *phitt*, also a chattering reel. HABITS: More skulking and warbler-like than other flycatchers, but makes serial sallies after insects. MAY BE CONFUSED with 83, 84, and (male) with 89.

Kinglet family: very small greenish birds, arboreal and insecti-vorous, often accompanying tit flocks, but attached to conifers. Sexes almost alike.

60 **Goldcrest,** *Regulus regulus*. Resident and passage migrant. Woodland, gardens, and parks, particularly where there are conifers. DESCRIPTION: 3½ inches. Sexes differ slightly. Wings have darker band with two pale bars. Male's crest orange-cen-tred, yellow in female, absent in juvenile. VOICE: Call *zee zee zee*, higher and shriller than similar calls of tits. Song, also very high, is superficially like that of 45. HABITS: Usually seen continuous-ly on move amongst higher branches of a conifer, but sometimes comes low and is indifferent to man. Round-winged fluttering flight between trees. MAY BE CONFUSED with 61, 62, 63, 65.

61 **Firecrest,** *Regulus ignicapillus*. Winter visitor and passage mi-grant, mainly to east and south-east; breeds several southern counties, especially Hants (New Forest). DESCRIPTION: 3½ in-ches. Sexes almost alike. Resembles 60 but crown streak fiery orange and black eyestripe with white stripes above and below

are distinctive. Plumage generally cleaner-looking than 60.
VOICE: Call as 60, but distinctly lower-pitched. HABITS: Less
confined to conifers than 60, but otherwise much the same.
MAY BE CONFUSED with 60, 65.

Warbler family: small to very small insectivorous birds, sexes
usually alike. Mostly summer visitors and divided into several
groups: **leaf warblers** (62–5) little greenish birds which spend most
of their time in the foliage; **river warblers** (66–9) brownish, rather
fan-tailed birds with loud songs but generally secretive habits;
typical warblers (71–6) rather long-tailed birds with fine songs,
found in woodland undergrowth and scrub.

62 **Chiffchaff,** *Phylloscopus collybita.* Summer visitor (end March
but a few resident in south-west) and passage migrant, local in
south Scotland, recently spreading into Highlands. Woodland
edge, spinneys, copses, and low scrub. DESCRIPTION: 4 inches.
Sexes alike. Legs blackish (a useful point). Juveniles browner.
VOICE: Usually recognized by two note song which gives
name; sometimes introduced by two grating notes. Call-note
hwit, uttered with varying emphasis and less drawn-out than
same note of 63. HABITS: Searches foliage for insects, often high
up and very seldom seen on ground. Short bursts of round-
winged flight. MAY BE CONFUSED with 60, 63 (especially), 64,
65.

63 **Willow Warbler,** *Phylloscopus trochilus.* Summer visitor (early
April) and passage migrant to open woodland and scrub of all
types. DESCRIPTION: 4 inches. Sexes alike. Considered to be
greener-looking than 62, but not safe to identify on plumage
unless legs can be clearly seen. Appears yellower in autumn and
juveniles distinctly so. Legs pale brown (a good point). VOICE:
Call-note *hweet* more sustained than 62 and can be distinguished
with practice. Song quite distinct: a tinkling cadence, resembling
song of 21 in form but without final flourish. HABITS: Much as
62. Juveniles seen on ground in late summer, when they hop.
MAY BE CONFUSED with 60, 62 (especially), 64, 65.

64 **Wood Warbler,** *Phylloscopus sibilatrix.* Summer visitor (mid-
April), local in south-east, becoming widespread in west and
north Britain; has bred in Ireland. Woods of beech, oak, ash,
and birch with little or no undergrowth. DESCRIPTION: 5
inches. Sexes alike. A larger and much 'cleaner' bird than 62

and 63. Note yellow stripe over eye. Juveniles and autumn adults duller. VOICE: Call-note penetrating plaintive *peee* rather like call of 18. Two songs: explosive trilling burst of surprising volume for so small bird, and repeated *piu piu piu* like song of 51. HABITS: Less restless than relatives but similar in movements and only visits ground when going to nest. Sallies after insects like a flycatcher. MAY BE CONFUSED with 62, 63.

65 **Yellow-browed Warbler,** *Phylloscopus inornatus.* Rare passage migrant, mainly east coast. DESCRIPTION: 4 inches. Sexes alike. Two pale wing-bars enclosing dark band and pale stripe over eye. VOICE: Call-note like that of 63 but sharper and louder. HABITS: Said to be more like 60 than other leaf-warblers. Aerial flights like flycatcher. MAY BE CONFUSED with 60, 61, 62, 63.

66 **Grasshopper Warbler,** *Locustella naevia.* Summer visitor (mid-April), widespread, but scarcer Scotland. Low thick cover: riverside marshes and bogs, young plantations and low scrub. DESCRIPTION: 5 inches. Sexes alike. An extremely mouse-like bird with rather long and conspicuously fanned tail. VOICE: Continuous thin reeling song; often at night. Volume appears to change due to bird turning head continually. Also sharp *chick* call-note. HABITS: Very secretive, but sometimes sings openly on a spray. When flushed flips up and quickly down again. MAY BE CONFUSED with 67, and with **Savi's Warbler** *Locustella luscinioides,* which now nests south-east England.

67 **Sedge Warbler,** *Acrocephalus schoenobaenus.* Summer visitor (mid-April), usually to thick cover near water, but sometimes in scrub some distance away. DESCRIPTION: 5 inches. Sexes alike. Rather like 66 but with prominent pale stripe over eye. Tail more rufous. Juveniles brighter looking than adults. VOICE: Call-notes grating *churr* and a staccato *tuck*. Song, often at night, a jumble of notes, rapidly delivered and often including sparrow-like chattering and notes of other birds. HABITS: Shows itself quite freely and sings from exposed perches, but also travels silently through vegetation. Song flights, soon after arrival, show rufous tail well. MAY BE CONFUSED with 66, 68 (chiefly because of similar habitat).

68 **Reed Warbler,** *Acrocephalus scirpaceus.* Summer visitor (late April), general to local in southern half Britain up to Cumbria. Reed-beds, osier-beds and other waterside vegetation.

DESCRIPTION: 5 inches. Sexes alike. About the size and shape of 67 but uniform unstreaked brown above. VOICE: Call-note churring, like 67. Song more regular, less harsh than 67, and based on two phrases alternating: *churr churr churr, churruck churruck churruck*. HABITS: Keeps very much to reeds and sings less from exposed perches than 67, but can be seen with patience. Nests socially. Short flights with tail hanging. MAY BE CONFUSED with 67, 69.

69 **Marsh Warbler,** *Acrocephalus palustris*. Summer visitor (May), confined to Severn and neighbouring valleys and to a few localities in southern England. Osier-beds with rank growth of nettles and other tall herbs. DESCRIPTION: 5 inches. Sexes alike. Almost indistinguishable from 68 but legs much lighter and lacks rufous tinge in upper parts. VOICE: Call and alarm notes much as 67 but less harsh. Song considered far superior to 67 and 68 and noted for mimicry, especially of 79. Repeated nasal *za-wee* is characteristic. HABITS: Much as relatives, but sings from high, exposed perches as well as from cover. MAY BE CONFUSED with 67, 68.

70 **Icterine Warbler,** *Hippolais icterina*. Rare passage migrant, mostly east and south coasts. Has bred once. DESCRIPTION: 5 inches. Sexes alike. Like big leaf-warbler, but shape more as 73. VOICE: Call-notes, a hard *tack* like that of 74 and a musical *dididid*. Varied song, rather like 69. HABITS: Keeps much to foliage and seldom lands on ground. Rather faltering moth-like flight. MAY BE CONFUSED with 64 and with Melodious Warbler *Hippolais polyglotta*, another rare passage migrant.

71 **Dartford Warbler,** *Sylvia undata*. Resident, confined to parts of a few southern counties. Heathland, usually with gorse bushes. DESCRIPTION: 5 inches. Sexes rather alike. Appears a very dark little bird in field, shaped like a small whitethroat. Upper parts of female and juvenile lighter, breast much more orange-brown than red. VOICE: Usual calls soft churr and staccato *tuck*, which can be told from similar notes of 75. Song a short musical warble, rather like 75. HABITS: Keeps very much to cover, but bobs up from time to time and may sing from quite exposed and lofty perches. Flies away usually with tail trailing and just clearing vegetation. MAY BE CONFUSED with 75.

72 **Barred Warbler,** *Sylvia nisoria*. Rare passage migrant, mainly to east coast. DESCRIPTION: 6 inches. Sexes differ somewhat.

Biggest warbler likely to be met with. White outer tail-feathers. Females and juveniles browner and less barred than male (as shown). VOICE: Usual churring and *tuck* notes of typical warblers; also a loud chatter. HABITS: Skulking in thick cover, with rather heavy flight when flushed. Seldom on ground where it hops. MAY BE CONFUSED (especially females and juveniles) with 55, 73.

73 **Garden Warbler,** *Sylvia borin*. Summer visitor (late April), general to central Scotland; very local Ireland. Woodland and woodland edge with bramble growth; young plantations. DESCRIPTION: 5½ inches. Sexes alike. Typical 'small brown bird': absence of any streaks, stripes, or other features is, in fact, quite distinctive. VOICE: *Tuck* call and churr lower but more forceful and penetrating than 74. Juveniles have distinct loud call-note. Song resembles 74, but typically much less jerky, more continuous and rippling as if it would never stop. HABITS: Shy and difficult to see, keeping even more to cover than 74. Seldom seen in flight. MAY BE CONFUSED with 72, 74 (especially on voice).

74 **Blackcap,** *Sylvia atricapilla*. Summer visitor (early April); some in winter every year; very local Ireland and mainly southern Scotland. Woodland and woodland edge with or without thick undergrowth; large gardens and parks. DESCRIPTION: 5½ inches. Sexes differ. Much greyer than 73. VOICE: Staccato *tuck tuck* is commonest note, but also churrs. Song a series of loud, rather jerky phrases of warbling notes, each burst ending abruptly. Mimics other birds. HABITS: Less retiring than 73 and sometimes sings from exposed perches, but for much of season only located by its song and call-notes. Looks grey when flushed into short flights. MAY BE CONFUSED with 73 and with black-headed tits, especially 50, when it appears in winter on bird-tables.

75 **Common Whitethroat,** *Sylvia communis*. Summer visitor (mid-April) to hedgerows and lanes, low scrub including heathland. DESCRIPTION: 5½ inches. Sexes differ slightly. A slim long-tailed warbler with white outer feathers. Female (not shown) and juvenile have brown heads. VOICE: Harsh *churr* most frequent note, but also *tuck tuck*. Rapid scratchy song represented as *chewichet chewichet chewichet* but sometimes almost as musical as 73. HABITS: Although spending much time in cover, shows itself far more than relatives, and often sings

from telegraph wires and other prominent perches or in flight. Constantly raises tail almost at right angles to body; also raises feathers of crown. MAY BE CONFUSED with 71, 76.

76 **Lesser Whitethroat,** *Sylvia curruca.* Summer visitor (second half April), local in northern England; has bred Scotland, Man but not Ireland. Bushy hedgerows overgrown with trailing plants and often with much blackthorn; commons with similar big bushes. DESCRIPTION: 5 inches. Sexes alike. Rather smaller and rather greyer-looking than 75 but best distinction dark mask, contrasting with lighter grey head. Under parts less pink. VOICE: *Tuck tuck* like 74 is commonest call, but has *churr* as well. Song rather explosive rattle, recalling song of 26, often as burst in continuous quiet warbling and squeaking notes. HABITS: Much more retiring than 75 and usually sings from cover, often high in trees. Otherwise resembles 75. MAY BE CONFUSED with 75.

Thrush family: a varied group of medium to small birds which eat berries, insects, worms, snails etc. Sexes often distinct. Some summer and some social winter visitors. Usually rather conspicuous with loud alarm calls and fine songs. Flight usually fairly direct.

77 **Fieldfare,** *Turdus pilaris.* Winter visitor to open farming country often to 1,000 ft. or more. Has bred mainly north Scotland. DESCRIPTION: 10 inches. Sexes alike. Most richly coloured thrush with prominent grey rump and black tail. VOICE: Loud *chack chack chack* calls from flocks or single birds, also a high musical *hweek.* HABITS: Arrives autumn and stays in large flocks, feeding over fields and gathering in hedgerow trees; also feeds on berries while they last. Nervous of human approach but can be seen closely from car. Birds move over fields from cover of hedge in little hopping rushes, stopping to look up before pecking at ground. MAY BE CONFUSED with 78, 79, 80.

78 **Mistle Thrush,** *Turdus viscivorus.* Resident in woodland edge, shelter-belts, parks, and gardens well into towns. DESCRIPTION: 10½ inches. Sexes alike. Biggest, bulkiest thrush: much greyer than 79 with pale outer tail-feathers. Scaly-looking juveniles mistaken for rare White's Thrush, *Zoothera dauma.* VOICE: Loud 'football fan's rattle' call is distinctive. Song a short phrase of fine fluting notes which can at distance be confused with 82.

HABITS: Pairs normally solitary and aggressive but parties and flocks form in autumn and cause confusion with 77. Flight a series of big bounds ending in sweep up to perch, usually high and prominent. Feeds mainly on ground except in berry season. MAY BE CONFUSED with 77, 79, 80, and (in flight) 101; also with very rare Nutcracker, *Nucifraga caryocatactes*.

79 **Song Thrush,** *Turdus philomelos.* Resident, summer and winter visitor and passage migrant. All types of cover from woodland to rocky moorland. DESCRIPTION: 9 inches. Sexes alike. Olive-brown upper parts; bright orange on flanks and under wings. VOICE: Call-note, used much in flight, is sibilant *seep*; also *chuck chuck* of alarm, less violent than that of 82. Song, one of the finest and most varied in Britain, consists of vigorous repetition of certain phrases, e.g. *katy-did*, with pauses between each burst; *piu* notes reminiscent of 88 quite frequent and may lead to confusion when Song Thrush sings late. Some mimicry of other birds. HABITS: Thrushes hopping about a lawn in search of food are familiar sight, but appetite for snails is distinctive and these are broken on regular anvils of stone or metal. Song perches often prominent. Plump silhouette in flight which is much more direct than 78. Parties and flocks of immigrants in winter. MAY BE CONFUSED with 55 (female), 77, 78, 80, 82 (female and juvenile).

80 **Redwing,** *Turdus iliacus.* Winter visitor, found in open woodland, farmland, parks, and big gardens, coastal dunes. Now breeds north Scotland. DESCRIPTION: 8 inches. Sexes alike. Darker and smaller than 79, with darker face, long pale stripe over eye and almost crimson flanks. VOICE: Call-note a protracted *seep* more penetrating than 79. Also, especially at roosts, staccato *chick* or *chittuck*. In early spring flocks indulge in communal warbling, from which one bird occasionally breaks into full song *tew-i tew-i tew-i.* HABITS: First evidence in autumn usually call-notes heard at night. Flocks stay together all winter, feeding on fields or on berries; very susceptible to prolonged cold spells. Flight as 79. Large communal roosts. MAY BE CONFUSED with 77, 78, 79.

81 **Ring Ouzel,** *Turdus torquatus.* Summer visitor (end March) and passage migrant, local to common Devon and north-west of Severn-to-Humber line; very local Ireland. Rocky hillsides and moorland. DESCRIPTION: 9½ inches. Sexes differ. Female (not

shown) browner, scalier, and with narrower dirty white crescent. Juveniles lack crescent and resemble 82. VOICE: Loud *tack tack tack* like clattering of small stones. Usual song repeated piping *tew tew tew* carrying a long way. HABITS: Usually seen flying along rocky slope and perching, when wings catch light and look dusty brown. Parties feed on rowan berries in late summer; odd birds seen on passage in lowlands. MAY BE CONFUSED with 82 (especially males with white patches on neck).

82 **Blackbird,** *Turdus merula.* Resident and winter visitor; almost everywhere except high moorland. DESCRIPTION: 10 inches. Sexes differ. Males with varying amounts of white quite frequent. Young males have much browner wings and black or partly black bills. Juvenile much as female but lighter. VOICE: Chuckling call-note becomes complicated scream of alarm, or angry ticking scold. Mellow fluting song heard mainly March-June, though quiet warbling goes on through year. HABITS: Mixture of boldness and shyness; feeds much in open, where hops or runs and has social gatherings on grass early in mornings. But spends much time in cover, flying between bushes with half-spread tail. Longer flights rather direct with usual plump thrush outline and longish tail. MAY BE CONFUSED with 81 and (females and juveniles) 79.

83 **Wheatear,** *Oenanthe oenanthe.* Summer visitor (end March) and passage migrant, local in south-east, becoming common in parts of west and north. Rocky and scree country, sandy heaths and dunes, downland. DESCRIPTION: 6 inches. Sexes differ. Spring male unmistakable. Female (not shown) sandy brown instead of grey and has only trace of mask. Juvenile as female but with upper parts and breast heavily scaled. Male in autumn much as female. VOICE: Usual call-note *whit chuck chuck* like clacking of small stones. Attractive, vigorous song phrase incorporates musical and harsh notes with some imitations. HABITS: Like other chats perches prominently on stones and skylines. Continually on move by hopping, stopping to stand very upright. In short flights, white tail flickers and is bobbed up and down when at rest. May be confused (in autumn) with 84.

84 **Whinchat,** *Saxicola rubetra.* Summer visitor (second half April), local but widespread; very local Ireland. Heather and grass heaths, bracken slopes and young plantations, grassy bogs and riverside

fields. DESCRIPTION: 5 inches. Sexes differ. Male is small, dapper chat with white spots at base of tail. Female (not shown) lacks distinctive mask and has less white on wing; juveniles and male in autumn resemble her. VOICE: Scolding double tick note like 85, with softer introductory *tew;* also clicking and churring calls. Song a short, often imitative, warble, deceptively variable. HABITS: Perches constantly on topmost spray of bushes, flicking tail and wings, then dropping to ground where it hops. Aerial sallies after insects. Short-tailed whirring flight. MAY BE CONFUSED with 59, 83, 85.

85 **Stonechat,** *Saxicola torquata.* Resident, summer visitor, passage migrant, locally common western coastal areas and Ireland. Very local or absent inland and along east coast. Heather and gorse heaths, young plantations. DESCRIPTION: 5 inches. Sexes differ. Juvenile resembles female. Autumn male is duller but recognizably distinct. VOICE: Typical note *wheet tick tick* similar to, but more emphatic than, 84; also clicking call-note. Song a variable repetition of quite musical notes. HABITS: Much as 83. Stance notably upright when perched. MAY BE CONFUSED with 83 and (male) 89.

86 **Redstart,** *Phoenicurus phoenicurus.* Summer visitor (mid-April): local to common; sporadic in Ireland. Typically highland scrub-woods and stone wall country, but also in lowland old woods, parks, and riversides with pollarded trees. DESCRIPTION: 5½ inches. Sexes differ. Male unmistakable but duller in autumn. Juveniles scaly brown. VOICE: Call *hweet* like strong version of 62 and 63. Alarm: *hweet tick tick* resembles 85 but lacks stony quality. Song a brief 'introductory' warble, cut off short; also an excellent mimic. HABITS: Easy to see on first arrival in spring but restless and quick-moving. Tremulous movement of tail, which is worked up and down in alarm. Aerial sallies after insects and seldom on ground where it resembles 89. MAY BE CONFUSED with 87.

87 **Black Redstart,** *Phoenicurus ochruros.* Summer visitor (April), very local in southern Britain; winter visitor and passage migrant. Breeds mainly coastal towns and on one or two large power stations. DESCRIPTION: 5½ inches. Sexes differ. Young males greyer and have little or no white on wing. Females (not shown) lighter grey with no white on wing but never show any brown

as 86. Males duller in autumn. VOICE: Call-note, short *hwit* often introduces the *tick tick* of alarm, very like 86. Warbling song, rather like 90, often ends with rattle 'like small metal balls', which is quite distinctive. HABITS: Sings high on buildings and roofs, gables, etc, but collects food largely off ground where hops about like 89, a bird it replaces round houses on the Continent. Also makes aerial sallies and in general resembles 86. MAY BE CONFUSED with 86.

88 **Nightingale,** *Luscinia megarhynchos.* Summer visitor (mid-April), practically confined south and east of Severn-Humber line. Woodland, thickets, and spinneys with bramble cover. DESCRIPTION: 6½ inches. Sexes alike. A plump robin-like bird with a rufous (not red) tail and big black eye. VOICE: A soft call like 63 and a *tick* like 89; also a fierce scolding croak. Song a mixture of drawn out *pius*, deep *jugs*, and rich warbling, with great carrying power and by no means confined to night. HABITS: Very skulking and hard to see, usually near ground on which it largely feeds. Low, short fluttering flights. MAY BE CONFUSED with 86 (female), 89.

89 **Robin,** *Erithacus rubecula.* Resident, summer visitor and passage migrant. Gardens, woodland, lanes, and banks. DESCRIPTION: 5½ inches. Sexes alike. Juvenile has buff spotted plumage till autumn. VOICE: Usual note irritable *tick tick*; call a thin *tseee*. Song a simple warble, slightly different in autumn, delivered with rather a burst, then dying away. HABITS: Familiar, confiding visitor to bird-table, often entering house. Moves on ground with pronounced hops, fluttering to cover when disturbed. Song-perches often exposed. MAY BE CONFUSED with 85 (male), 88.

Accentor family: Only one common species in Britain.

90 **Dunnock or Hedge Sparrow,** *Prunella modularis.* Resident in almost all types of low and fairly dry cover. DESCRIPTION: 6 inches. Sexes alike. Predominantly grey head with thin bill distinguishes from 30. VOICE: Call a single penetrating *tseep;* also rapid whickering note uttered in thick cover. Song a sudden simple warbling phrase much more abrupt than 89 and less forceful and rattling than 91; sometimes uttered at night. HABITS: Retiring by nature but often sings openly and feeds on bare

patches, with low hopping action. Agitated flicking of wings and tail characteristic. MAY BE CONFUSED with 30 (female).

Wren family: Only one species in Britain.

91 **Wren,** *Troglodytes troglodytes.* Resident (distinct races Shetland, Hebrides, St Kilda), everywhere except bare moorland and town centres. DESCRIPTION: 4 inches. Sexes alike. Unique shape with up-turned tail. VOICE: Repeated staccato ticking note with 'machine-gun' and churring variants. Song an explosive rattling warble. HABITS: A fussy, mouse-like bird, expert at moving in thick vegetation, at times appearing to view with cocked-up tail, then darting off. Rapid whirring flight, often for hundred yards or more. Often roosts communally, tens of birds together, in cavity or nestbox.

Dipper family: only one species in Britain.

92 **Dipper,** *Cinclus cinclus.* Resident (distinct race in Ireland), general in west and north; absent or very rare south and east of Severn-Humber line, away from fast-flowing waters. DES-CRIPTION: 7 inches. Sexes alike. VOICE: Call a carrying *dip dip* used at rest and, slightly varied, in flight. Song a continuous babbling warble, an epitome of the water by which it is uttered. HABITS: Dipping action when perched on boulders in stream. Swims, dives, and walks on bottom expertly. Swift, low whirring flight but occasionally rockets high overhead.

Swallow family: small summer visitors with forked tails, feeding in the air on flying insects and seldom landing on ground. Sexes alike.

93 **Swallow,** *Hirundo rustica.* Summer visitor (from early April) to farms, small holdings, riversides, suburbia. DESCRIPTION: 7½ inches (including tail). White spots on tail show in flight. Juveniles have much shorter streamers, are duller and hard to tell from 94 in silhouette. VOICE: Call notes *twit twit twit* run into twittering warble of song. Also a single, drawn out *tsweet* of alarm. HABITS: Spends hours on wing, hawking for insects, but also rests on wires, buildings, sometimes trees. Clumsy walk when it lands. Sings on wing or perched. Autumn gatherings,

often with 94 and 95 characteristic, and then roosts communally, often in reed-beds. MAY BE CONFUSED (especially juveniles) with 94, 95, 96.

94 **House Martin,** *Delichon urbica.* Summer visitor (mid April) to habitations, farms, some inland and sea cliffs. DESCRIPTION: 5 inches. Sexes alike. Tail fork much blunter than 93 and head rounder-looking. Juveniles browner above. VOICE: Continuous chittering calls interspersed with *tsweet* of alarm, both much gentler than 93. Song, rather seldom heard, a development of the chitter. HABITS: Like 93, but noticeable when flying up to eaves and when gathering mud for nest at roadside puddles. Strongly colonial when nesting and social at all times. MAY BE CONFUSED with 93, 95, 96.

95 **Sand Martin,** *Riparia riparia.* Summer visitor (early April), widespread, but local in some highland areas. Riverside banks, sandpits, and gravel pits. DESCRIPTION: 5 inches. Sexes alike. Smaller than 94 with short forked tail. VOICE: A pebbly chatter interspersed by harsh alarm note. Song only a development of the chatter. HABITS: Much as relatives, which all hunt over water, but parties flying about close together are frequent. Often settles on ground or in vegetation. Colonial when nesting and social at all times. MAY BE CONFUSED with 93, 94, 96.

NEAR-PASSERINE BIRDS

After the great Passerine Order are grouped several orders of medium-sized, often brightly coloured birds, poorly represented in Britain. Only the **Woodpeckers** have more than one common species; they are characterized by striking plumage, sexes usually slightly different, by 'bounding' flight and by arrangement of toes: two forward and two back, which enables them to grip trees for climbing, supporting themselves also by stiff tails.

96 **Swift,** *Apus apus.* Summer visitor (early May) and passage migrant. Neighbourhood of towns and villages, possibly some inland cliffs; ranges widely from nesting places. DESCRIPTION: $6\frac{1}{2}$ inches. Sexes alike. Very long curved wings distinguish it from 93, 95. Juveniles look scaly. VOICE: Usual call-note is wild scream, becoming sustained squeal during aerial

chases. HABITS: Rapid dashing flight and cross-bow silhouette characteristic. Soon after arrival, mad aerial chases take place. Feeding flights at great heights and on tops of hills, birds skimming just above the ground. Seldom lands on ground, but clings to masonry and crawls into nests. Colonial and social at all times. MAY BE CONFUSED with 93, 94, 95.

97 **Nightjar,** *Caprimulgus europaeus.* Summer visitor, widespread but local in open uncultivated country: felled woods, heaths, commons, dunes, bracken slopes. DESCRIPTION: 10½ inches. Sexes differ somewhat. A long-tailed, long-winged, round-headed bird with wonderful mottled plumage. Male has white spots on wings and on tips of outer tail-feathers. VOICE: Churring or reeling at dusk or early in morning, much more powerful and lower pitched than reel of 66. Sustained for several minutes with variations in volume as bird turns head. Call of male *quick*, often repeated. HABITS: Flies at dusk silently, twisting and turning after moths and insects; also remarkable display flights with wing-clapping by male. When flushed in day-time from ground settles again quickly, sometimes on tree, perching along branch.

98 **Hoopoe,** *Upupa epops.* Scarce passage migrant, most records in southern England; has bred. Usually appears in gardens, allotments, and farm crops. DESCRIPTION: 11 inches (bill, 2). Sexes alike. Unmistakable if seen close; in flight very round barred wings and white band across black on tail show up. Crest normally flat, not as shown. HABITS: Often seen in Britain probing on lawns, walking easily. When flushed rises and flaps off like a huge moth. MAY BE CONFUSED (in flight) with 7.

99 **Roller,** *Coracias garrulus.* Rare visitor; most records east and south England near coast in rather open wooded country. DESCRIPTION: 12 inches. Sexes alike. Juveniles duller. HABITS: May perch in open on tree or wires, taking insects in air or dropping to ground where it hops like a crow. Flight described as 'easy and buoyant'.

100 **Kingfisher,** *Alcedo atthis.* Resident, except north Scotland, by slow flowing streams and rivers with high banks; by lakes and even by sea outside breeding season. DESCRIPTION: 6½ inches (bill 1½). Sexes alike. Quite unmistakable. VOICE: Call in flight loud *chrit* or *chrikee*; several other notes recorded, also

whistling which is seldom heard. HABITS: Usually seen as brilliant blue flash flying low over water with wings whirring fast. Perches motionless on overhanging branch or hovers before diving on to prey.

101 **Green Woodpecker,** *Picus viridis.* Resident, general England and Wales; spreading in Scotland, absent Ireland. Open wooded country, not thick woods. DESCRIPTION: $12\frac{1}{2}$ inches. Sexes almost alike. Green plumage with bright yellow rump and red cap take the eye. Juvenile duller, with streaks and spots. VOICE: The laugh or 'yaffle', with variations, is characteristic: a bird's imitation of a horse neighing. HABITS: Usually seen in flight which consists of enormous bounds, dropping with closed wings and rising again. Feeds much on grassland, hopping and then standing almost upright. Roosts in holes. MAY BE CONFUSED (chiefly in flight) with 10, 78.

102 **Lesser Spotted Woodpecker,** *Dendrocopos minor.* Resident, widespread in England and Wales. Woodland (not conifers), parks, large gardens, and orchards. DESCRIPTION: 6 inches. Sexes differ somewhat. A little larger than 44 with conspicuously barred black and white upperparts. Crown crimson in male, brownish white in female (not shown). Juvenile much as female. VOICE: Loud high *pee pee pee . . .* may be confused with similar calls of 44 and 104. Less common is *blick* note like 103. HABITS: Actions like other woodpeckers, but owing to size seen more on twigs and often with flocks of tits. In spring drums on dead wood, a reverberating beat carrying a long way and not much feebler than 103. MAY BE CONFUSED with 103.

103 **Great Spotted Woodpecker,** *Dendrocopos major.* Resident (some winter visitors of northern race), England, Wales, local to north Scotland; but not Ireland or Man. Woodlands and wooded country but not thick conifers. DESCRIPTION: 9 inches. Sexes differ somewhat. Not only much larger than 102, but plumage not barred except on flight-feathers; two conspicuous areas of white on back when at rest. Only male has crimson back of head but juveniles have red caps. VOICE: Usual note a loud staccato *blick*, sometimes repeated. Young buzz loudly in nest-hole. HABITS: Much as other woodpeckers; seldom on ground. Drums chiefly in spring, usually on wood but sometimes on metal caps of telegraph poles.

Bounding flight not so exaggerated as 101. MAY BE CON-
FUSED with 102.

104 Wryneck, *Jynx torquilla.* Summer visitor now confined to
extreme south-east England, but nested Scottish Highlands
1969, possibly 1970; regular on passage along east coast. Open
wooded country, especially orchards and large gardens.
DESCRIPTION: 6½ inches. Sexes alike. A bird of curiously
individual shape: thin, almost snake-like, with beautifully
variegated plumage. Back of head looks 'crew cut'. VOICE:
Call and song is ringing *quee* repeated many times and
resembling similar calls of 44, 102, 112. HABITS: Secretive,
usually revealed by call. Perches across twigs, clings to trunks
like woodpecker and often lands on ground where it hops with
raised tail. Remarkable twisting of neck, especially when
alarmed. Flapping, dipping flight.

105 Cuckoo, *Cuculus canorus.* Summer visitor, wherever chief
fosterers are found (e.g. 37, 68, 90). DESCRIPTION: 13 inches.
Sexes almost alike. Female has brownish collar effect, and there is
'hepatic' variety (as shown) with all upperparts barred brown.
Juveniles resemble this, but are dark brown with scaling on back.
VOICE: *Cuckoo* normally only from male; female has bubbling
call impossible to represent. HABITS: Rather secretive, though
may be seen cuckooing early in season and often perches openly
on wires etc. over Meadow Pipit habitats. Walks badly or hops
on ground. Flies straight, pointed wings moving fast; some
similarity to hawk, but flat-looking head, small bill and rounded throat destroy illusion. MAY BE CONFUSED with 114, 115,
123.

OWL ORDER

Medium to large birds of prey, usually of nocturnal habits and with
round 'facial discs'. Sexes alike. Plumage variegated, often in shades
of brown, feathers constructed for silent flapping flight.

106 Snowy Owl *Nyctea scandiaca.* Rare visitor, mainly to north
Scotland. Has bred Shetland since 1967. Open moorland, marshes and dunes. DESCRIPTION: 21-24 inches. Sexes differ and female much larger. Barred effect much more pronounced in
females; old males almost pure white. VOICE: Usually silent,
but has a loud crowing shriek. HABITS: Usually seen in hard

weather, hunting much by day like a large hawk. Settles freely on stones and ground. MAY BE CONFUSED with 111.

107 **Little Owl,** *Athene noctua*. Introduced resident, general in England and Wales and has now reached Scotland. Mainly farming country; not moors, marshes, thick woods, or towns. DESCRIPTION: 8½–9 inches. Sexes alike. A small liver-brown owl with pale spots and streaks on upper parts. Very dumpy and round-winged in flight. VOICE: Usual notes, a burst of yelping shrieks or a rather sad cry of two notes, reminiscent of Curlew's call. Many other noises recorded. HABITS: Perches in open in daylight, often seen as squat huddled shape against telegraph poles, and makes sudden bounding flights, almost like 78 and often accompanied by mobbing chorus from small birds. If hungry, hunts in daylight and often at dusk, when hovering recorded.

108 **Long-eared Owl,** *Asio otus*. Resident and winter visitor, local but widespread, commoner in Scotland and Ireland. Woodland, especially conifer belts. DESCRIPTION: 13½ inches. Sexes alike. A rather slender owl, with beautiful mottled plumage. Ear tufts prominent when at rest but flat in flight. Fierce yellow eye. VOICE: Moaning hoot with spaced out syllables is most characteristic call; also noise very like dog barking in distance; many other notes recorded. HABITS: Retiring woodland owl, roosting close to tree trunks but betrayed by ring of pellets and droppings below. In flight looks more slender than 110, greyer and rounder-winged than 109, but difficult to tell apart in poor light. MAY BE CONFUSED with 109, 110.

109 **Short-eared Owl,** *Asio flammeus*. Resident, local to very local; does not breed Ireland. Winter visitors fairly widespread. Extensive open areas, especially grass moors, young plantations, bogs, marshes, and dunes. DESCRIPTION: 14½ inches. Sexes alike. General appearance as 108, but browner and longer-winged; ear tufts hardly show. VOICE: Hooting song in display and barks when nest is threatened. HABITS: Distinguished from other 'brown' owls by habitat (though 108 occasionally in open country) and by regular daylight hunting. Looks more like harrier than owl on wing with slow, long-winged beats and glides, often skimming over ground. Perches on posts, stones, etc., horizontally like hawk, not upright like owl.

Sometimes several together in winter. MAY BE CONFUSED with 108, 110, 120, 121.

110 **Tawny Owl,** *Strix aluco.* Resident in Britain, absent Ireland and most islands. Woodland and wooded country including town parks and gardens. DESCRIPTION: 15 inches. Sexes alike. By far stoutest looking of 'brown' owls with large round head; big black eye distinguishes from 108 and 109 at close quarters. A grey form occurs occasionally. VOICE: Male's call is traditional *tu-whit tu-whoo;* hunting call *kee-wit* also commonly heard. Young have rather distinct form of this. HABITS: Nocturnal, but often discovered at daylight roost by mobbing of small birds. Seen in dark on telegraph poles, buildings, and other prominent perches. Care advised when visiting nests as this is easily fiercest of British birds, attacking silently in dive from above. MAY BE CONFUSED with 108, 109, and (in flight) 186.

111 **Barn Owl,** *Tyto alba.* Resident, widespread, but old buildings in farmland favoured. DESCRIPTION: 13½ inches. Sexes alike. White appearance distinguishes from all owls except very rare and much bigger 106. At close range beautifully mottled upperparts obvious, but speckling on breast not visible in field. VOICE: The 'screech' owl – usually uttered in flight and has blood-curdling almost human quality. Also *kee-wit* like 110 but less forceful. Young in nest purr or 'snore' loudly. HABITS: Hunts in daylight when food scarce, e.g. late winter, or when feeding young. At such times also perches in open but usually roosts in cavities and presence may go undetected unless searched for. MAY BE CONFUSED with 106.

HAWK ORDER

Medium to very large birds of prey, divided into several groups. Those with more than one British member are: **Falcons** (112–15) – sharp-winged, long-tailed, brown-eyed; sexes somewhat distinct and females bigger; hunt by diving ('stooping') on prey or by flying it down; **Eagles** and **Buzzards** (116–18) large, round-winged, brown-eyed; sexes alike but females usually bigger; plumage brownish, variable; much given to soaring and gliding; hunt by dropping on prey; **Harriers** (119–21) – resemble falcons, but longer-legged and yellow-eyed; sexes distinct, plumage variable; flapping and gliding flight; hunt by quartering ground and dropping; **Sparrowhawks** (122-3) – round-winged, yellow-eyed; sexes rather alike but females much bigger; hunt by swift surprise.

112 **Kestrel,** *Falco tinnunculus.* Resident, winter visitor and passage migrant, even to city centres. DESCRIPTION: 13-14 inches. Sexes differ. Distinguished from other hawks of comparable size by light chestnut upperparts. Female (not shown) is fairly uniformly barred chestnut-brown above. Juveniles resemble female. See also p. 222. VOICE: Usual call a repeated chattering scream, varying a good deal in intensity and at times to be confused with calls of 44, 102, 104; sometimes only a single syllable. HABITS: Most commonly seen British hawk, flying with swift beats then stopping to hover with winnowing wings and tail spread fanlike to balance; drops like stone from hover to ground. Uses exposed perches of all kinds. MAY BE CONFUSED with 114, 115, 123, 181.

113 **Peregrine,** *Falco peregrinus.* Resident and passage migrant, much decreased in recent years, but still found in north and west; especially Central Scotland. Near crags and sea cliffs; in winter coastal marshes and estuaries but may occur anywhere. DESCRIPTION: 15 (male) to 19 (female) inches. Sexes differ somewhat. A big falcon with bow-shaped silhouette, tail relatively short and almost pointed. Upper parts darker grey and underparts more heavily marked in female. Juveniles similar in pattern but dark brown and have heavily streaked underparts. See also p. 222. VOICE: Repeated ringing screams, far stronger than 112, used near nest; a single cry may be call note. HABITS: Usually seen in flight, a series of rapid beats alternating with glides; from certain angles not unlike a pigeon. Pursues prey or 'stoops' (dives) from above at great speed. Perches openly when white breast stands out at long distance. MAY BE CONFUSED with pigeons in flight; (male) with 114.

114 **Hobby,** *Falco subbuteo.* Summer visitor (early May), very local in southern England. Open woodland, pine clumps, and tall hedges. DESCRIPTION: 12 (male) to 14 (female) inches. Sexes alike except for size. Miniature 113, but outline even more like 96, with long sharp wings and a shortish tail. Juveniles dark

brown above, lack crimson on flanks. See also p. 222. VOICE: Repeated call resembles that of 112 but can be distinguished with practice, although it has many variants. Also a single high-pitched note. HABITS: Usually seen in rapid flight like large 96 and soars amongst Swallows and Swifts; hunts like 113, also going low after insects, especially dragonflies. Perches on trees and is difficult to see at rest. MAY BE CONFUSED with 105, 112, 113, 115.

115 Merlin, *Falco columbarius.* Resident and winter visitor, breeds locally in west and north, probably decreasing. Moorland of drier types; in winter generally in open country. DESCRIPTION: $10\frac{1}{2}$ (male) to 13 (female) inches. Sexes differ. Male easily smallest of commoner hawks. Much larger female (not shown) is dark brown above with underparts heavily streaked; juveniles like female. See also p. 222. VOICE: Rather silent but has usual repeated falcon shriek near nest and single note call. HABITS: Perhaps most beautiful flier of all the hawks, very light with a tripping action as though continually changing step; quick wing-beats alternate with glides. Hunts mainly by pursuit. Uses exposed perches on rocks etc. MAY BE CONFUSED with 105, 112, 114, 123.

116 Golden Eagle, *Aquila chrysaetos.* Resident Scottish Highlands and Islands, Galloway; single pair Lake District since 1969; N. Ireland 1953-60. Moorland and mountainous country, also sea cliffs. DESCRIPTION: 30-35 inches (female larger). Sexes alike. Juvenile (as shown) has white base to black tail and shows white on wing, leading to confusion with 125. Conversely, immature 125 has dark tail and may be confused with adults of this species. But tail of 125 always relatively short compared to wings. Head, wings, and tail of this species look relatively longer than 118 and beak is more powerful. See also p. 223. VOICE: Usually silent but has yelping, barking and whistling calls. HABITS: Usually seen as majestic silhouette soaring high against hills, when spread flight feathers are characteristic. Hunts rather low, flying its prey down. Walks clumsily and frequently perches on skyline look-out. MAY BE CONFUSED with 118, 125.

117 Rough-legged Buzzard, *Buteo lagopus.* Rare winter visitor, mainly east coast and Pennines, in open country of all types. DESCRIPTION: 20-24 inches. Sexes alike but female generally larger. Very like 118 but distinguished by more or less white tail with dark brown terminal band underneath. Legs feathered. See also p. 223. VOICE: Catlike call much as 118. HABITS: Much as 118 but hovers more and habitat usually different. MAY BE CONFUSED with 118.

118 Common Buzzard, *Buteo buteo*. Resident, occasional winter visitor; now breeding in most of Scotland, Wales, western and locally southern England, and in N. Ireland since 1951. Moorland, sea-coasts and islands, wooded farming country especially if rather hilly. DESCRIPTION: 20–22 inches. Sexes alike but female usually larger. A big, dark brown, broad-winged hawk with extremely variable plumage, some birds showing a great deal of white (as much as 117), others very dark all over (as shown). Usually smaller and dumpier than 117 and bare yellow legs if they can be seen are distinctive. See also p. 223. VOICE: Usual call is loud but plaintive mew; sometimes in two syllables of which first is emphasized. Juveniles have a variation reminiscent of call of 210. HABITS: Generally seen in soaring flight or perched with humped silhouette on roadside tree or even telegraph pole. When flying with flight feathers spread looks very like 116, but often wing is bluntly pointed. Heavy flapping flight with glides like 119. Sometimes hovers above cliffs or steep hillsides and dives steeply. MAY BE CONFUSED with 116, 117, 119, 122, 124, 126, 127.

119 Marsh Harrier, *Circus aeruginosus*. Very rare resident East Anglia, occasionally breeds elsewhere. Extensive reed-beds near lakes or broads. DESCRIPTION: 19–22 inches. Sexes differ. Plumage most likely to be seen as top bird shown: females and young males. Some birds almost uniformly dark brown. See also p. 223. VOICE: Silent except in breeding season when both sexes have rather shrill calls. HABITS: Heavy flapping flight with glides can be confused with low-flying 118. Difficult to see on ground where it walks. MAY BE CONFUSED with 118, 120, and 121 (females), 129 (in flight).

120 Montagu's Harrier, *Circus pygargus*. Rare summer visitor (early May) to England, Wales; sporadic Ireland; has bred Scotland. Extensive open areas, especially moorland and very young plantations, reed-beds, and marshes. DESCRIPTION: 16–18 inches. Sexes differ. Much smaller and slimmer than 119 with narrow, pointed wings. Both sexes have small white rumps. See 121 for differences. Juveniles, though resembling females above, have rufous underparts which juvenile 121 has not. See also p. 223. VOICE: A loud repeated *kee* when near nest, very similar to 121. HABITS: Usually seen in flight, much lighter and more buoyant than 119 but has same characteristics of alternating beats and glide; wings much narrower than 109. Uses low perches often with horizontal stance. MAY BE CONFUSED with 109, 119, 121, 123.

121 **Hen Harrier,** *Circus cyaneus.* Resident Orkney, Scottish Highlands and Islands, several Irish, English and Welsh counties. Moorland; general in winter. DESCRIPTION: 17–20 inches. Sexes differ, female larger than male. Male much as 120, but no black wing-bar or streaks on underparts and white rump clearer and bigger. Female often has larger and whiter rump but not certainly distinguishable in field from 120. Juvenile as female. See also p. 223. VOICE: Rather silent, but has keeing call at nest like 120. HABITS: Much as 120, hunting low over ground and pouncing. Walks and hops with ease on ground. MAY BE CONFUSED with 109, 119, 120, 123.

122 **Goshawk,** *Accipiter gentilis.* Rare visitor, mainly east coast; now breeding regularly, possibly by falconers' escapes. Woodland of all types, especially conifers. DESCRIPTION: 19–23 inches. Sexes alike but female much larger. A big round-winged fan-tailed hawk with broad bars on tail. Juveniles have browner, spotted underparts. See also p. 222 VOICE: Usually silent but has buzzard-like mew near nest and piercing alarm notes typical of most hawks. HABITS: Very difficult to see except on soaring flights in display; ordinarily flies swiftly and silently amongst trees with beats and short glides. Plucking sites on tree stumps, etc., near nest. MAY BE CONFUSED with 118, 123.

123 **Sparrowhawk,** *Accipiter nisus.* Resident and passage migrant in wooded areas. DESCRIPTION: 11–15 inches. Sexes differ and female much larger. Male (not shown) has grey upper parts, and underparts closely barred rufous-brown; grey tail has broad darker bars. Both sexes may have pale patch on nape. Juveniles browner than adults, but all plumages variable. In flight appears much rounder-winged than 112 or other falcons,

see p. 222. VOICE: Shrieking alarm call; many other notes recorded at nest. HABITS: Typical hunting is mixture of beats and short glides skimming close to ground, or along hedges, then suddenly flipping over or dashing amongst flock of small birds; soaring flights in spring. Seldom seen on ground where usual gait is walk. MAY BE CONFUSED with 112, 115, 122.

124 **Red Kite,** *Milvus milvus.* Rare resident in small area of south central Wales. Hilly country with moorland and hanging woods of oak. DESCRIPTION: 24-25 inches. Sexes alike. Longer-winged than 118 and with clear-cut forked tail. Juveniles duller – less red. See also p. 223. VOICE: Occasionally utters buzzard-like but higher pitched mew. HABITS: Flies much as 118 but more gracefully and with more angle to wings; soars a great deal, using tail. Feeds mainly on ground where it hops. MAY BE CONFUSED with 118.

125 **Sea Eagle,** *Haliaeetus albicilla.* Rare visitor; most records now from south-east. Formerly bred Scotland; reintroduction attempted 1968. DESCRIPTION: 27-36 inches. Sexes alike but female usually larger. General resemblance to 116 but greater wing-span and shorter graduated tail distinguish at a distance, see p. 223. Adults have very light brown heads and white tails, but juveniles have dark tails. Legs yellow, not feathered; bill bigger than 116. HABITS: Heavy flapping flight with slightly bent wings, which are kept straight like vulture when soaring; often hunts low over water or land, snatching up prey. Perches prominently and spends much time at rest. MAY BE CONFUSED with 116.

126 **Honey Buzzard,** *Pernis apivorus.* Rare summer visitor mainly in southern England; a few pairs breed. Open woodland of various types. DESCRIPTION: 20-23 inches. Sexes alike. Resembles 118, but in flight wings and tail look longer in relation to body; see p. 223. VOICE: Usually silent, but has variously described call-note, quite distinct from and more sibilant than mewing of 118. HABITS: Soars like 118, but spends much more time on ground, running about freely, where it digs out wasps' nests and catches small animals. Bill held out straight in flight, not downwards as 118. MAY BE CONFUSED with 118.

127 **Osprey,** *Pandion haliaetus.* Rare passage migrant mainly on east side, including Scottish Highlands where several pairs now breed annually. Shallow lakes and lochs, often with prominent trees and islands. DESCRIPTION: 20–23 inches. Sexes alike but female usually larger. Another large buzzard-size hawk, but wings long and rather narrow with distinct kink; see p. 223. Noticeably long legs. VOICE: Usual call a thin repeated whistle but also a noisy alarm, variously rendered. HABITS: Almost always seen over or beside water, hunting by flapping and gliding and then plunging in after prey. Usual perch a prominent dead branch near water. MAY BE CONFUSED with 118.

HERON ORDER

Very large, very long-legged wading birds. Sexes alike. Legs stretched back in slow flapping flight. Breed socially but often solitary at other times.

128 **Heron,** *Ardea cinerea,* Resident in neighbourhood of water, especially river valleys and marshes, also sea-coast and even cliffs. DESCRIPTION: 36 inches (body 16). Sexes alike. In flight black underwing shows, neck is arched back and legs are held straight beyond tail. Juveniles greyer and more streaky. VOICE: Hoarse nasal *kwark* is usual call, but many notes recorded at nest. HABITS: Stands motionless in shallow water waiting to stab prey; head sunk in shoulders but neck raised on any alarm; walks slowly and deliberately. Often perches in trees, more or less exposed. In flight, slow heavy beats almost suggest large bird of prey. Nests socially and parties often seen together at all times.

129 **Bittern,** *Botaurus stellaris.* Rare resident East Anglian, Cumbrian reeds-beds but odd pairs elsewhere and in winter widespread. DESCRIPTION: 30 inches (body 14). Sexes alike. A rather dumpy heron-like bird with enormous elongation of neck. Neck held in and legs trail in flight. VOICE: Call note hoarse squawk, but most useful guide to presence of the bird is male's spring booming: a series of several hoots as of a miniature fog-horn and carrying a long way. HABITS: Usually remains hidden

in reeds, but sometimes appears in open, especially in winter. Also makes flights over reeds. Walks slowly and freezes with bill pointed upwards when alarmed. MAY BE CONFUSED in flight with 119.

130 **Spoonbill,** *Platalea leucorodia.* Rather rare visitor to coasts, especially east and south-east England and South Devon; formerly bred. DESCRIPTION: 34 inches (body 15). Sexes alike. Heronlike bird with almost all white plumage. Flies with neck and legs stretched. Juvenile has black wing tips. HABITS: Usually seen either resting with bill tucked behind, feeding by wading in shallow water and dredging from side to side, or in flight with slow wing-beats and occasional glides. MAY BE CONFUSED at a distance with 132 or with very rare herons.

DUCK ORDER

Large to very large water-birds with webbed feet and rather flattened bills. All have flightless moult period ('eclipse') in summer and many form large flocks outside breeding season. Divided into **swans** – very large, white, long-necked; sexes alike; feed by dabbling, up-ending, and grazing; **geese** – large to very large, long-necked, rather drab plumages; sexes alike; feed mainly by grazing; flocks ('skeins') fly in Vs with deceptively slow beats; **surface ducks** – medium to large, sharp-winged; males (drakes) brightly coloured; females (ducks) brownish; 'speculum' or coloured band on inner flight feathers often distinctive; wing-beats very fast; feed by dabbling, up-ending, and grazing; **diving** and **sea-ducks** – much as surface ducks but usually lack distinctive speculum and feed mainly by diving.

131 **Bewick's Swan,** *Cygnus bewickii.* Winter visitor, widespread but local, to sheltered coastal waters, lakes and floodwaters. DESCRIPTION: 48 inches (body 24). Sexes alike. Smaller than 132 with straighter, more gooselike neck; area of yellow on upper part of bill rounded off, not pointed as 132. Juveniles and immature birds grey or greyish, with pale bills showing the distinctive pattern. VOICE: Conversational notes on water change to loud but low-pitched honking in flight. HABITS:

Usually seen on water or in flight with necks stretched out and regular sweeping wing-beats. May graze on land. Generally in small parties, occasionally in large herds. MAY BE CONFUSED with 132, 133.

132 Whooper Swan, *Cygnus cygnus.* Winter visitor, commoner in Scotland and north England; has bred. Habitat as 131. DESCRIPTION: 60 inches (body 30). Sexes alike. Bigger than 131 and longer-necked; yellow area on bill extends to point at nostril. Juveniles and immatures greyish, but show bill pattern. VOICE: *Whooper* call on wing, a rather musical fluting double note. HABITS: Usually seen on water or in flight as 131, but comes to land at times and walks. Seen in any numbers from one to several hundred with distinct family units in each herd. MAY BE CONFUSED with 131, 133.

133 Mute Swan, *Cygnus olor.* Resident, partly tame; scarcer in Scotland. Lakes, ponds, rivers, even small streams; estuaries and other sheltered tidal waters. DESCRIPTION: 60 inches (body 30). Looks more massive than 132. Many birds show rusty heads from feeding in muddy water containing iron. Black knob at base of bill distinguishes from 131 and 132. Browny-grey juveniles and immatures have pale bills with traces of knob. VOICE: Snorts and hisses when alarmed. HABITS: Arching of wings over back when swimming is characteristic. In flight wings make musical hum audible a long way away. Walks on land and grazes a good deal as well as feeding in water. MAY BE CONFUSED with 130, 131, 132.

134 Greylag Goose, *Anser anser.* Rare resident in north-west Scotland and Hebrides; winter visitor mainly to central Scotland and parts of Ireland. Feral colonies established in several areas. Breeds heathery moorland with pools and lochs; in winter on farmland with water near; coastal marshes and estuaries. DESCRIPTION: 30–35 inches (body 20). Sexes alike. Biggest 'grey' goose, wild counterpart of the domestic bird. Actually grey-brown; white area around tail shows dark fan-shaped band in flight. Distinctive marks: pale grey-blue forewing and rump together with bright orange bill. Looks bigger headed and longer necked than 136 with which often seen. VOICE: as farmyard birds, a deep *honk-honk-honk.* HABITS: Wild geese usually seen in flight, with necks stretched and deceptively slow-looking wing-beats. They fly in regular

Vs when going any distance. On ground in 'gaggles' they look very like domestic birds but walk much more gracefully; typically some birds feed while several look round with necks straight. MAY BE CONFUSED with 135, 136, 137, 138.

135 **Bean Goose,** *Anser fabalis.* Scarce winter visitor, chiefly east England and south-west Scotland. Farmland near estuaries. DESCRIPTION: 28-35 inches (body 18–20). Dark-brown head, neck and upper parts contrast with paler underparts; generally looks darker than other 'grey' geese. Forewing dark. Pale margins to feathers often prominent. Tail pattern as 134. VOICE: Rather silent; honk resembles both 134 and 136. HABITS: Much as 134. MAY BE CONFUSED with 134, 136, 137, 138.

136 **Pink-footed Goose,** *Anser brachyrhynchus.* Winter visitor; regarded by some authorities as race of 135. Mainly east coast, and western estuaries from Clyde to Severn. Farmland near lochs and estuaries, but sometimes well inland. DESCRIPTION: 24-30 inches (body 17–19). Sexes alike. Looks smaller than 134 and distinguished from 135 by very dark brown head and neck but greyish upper parts; also by pale forewing in flight. Bill black and pink and noticeably small. VOICE: Honking higher pitched but similar to 134; can be distinguished with practice. HABITS: Much as 134 but in larger flocks. MAY BE CONFUSED with 134, 135, 137, 138.

137 **White-fronted Goose,** *Anser albifrons.* Winter visitor, widespread, but local and absent south-east England. Bogs, tidal marshes, and flooded land usually near coast, but sometimes far inland. DESCRIPTION: 26–30 inches (body 17–19). Sexes alike. Darker all over than 134 and 136, with black bars on underparts and prominent white blaze; forewing not distinct. Juveniles lack the barring and the blaze and are difficult to identify if alone. VOICE: Repeated laughing *honkly-onk* is quite distinctive. HABITS: Much as 134, but considered to have superior powers of manoeuvre in flight. MAY BE CONFUSED with 134, 135, 136, and especially 138.

138 **Lesser White-fronted Goose,** *Anser erythropus.* Rare winter visitor, mainly western estuaries, especially Severn. Habitat as 137. DESCRIPTION: 21–26 inches (body 16–17). Sexes alike. General resemblance to 137, but stubbier (noticeable in head),

darker, and longer-winged. Best distinctions: much more extensive white blaze and yellow ring round eye, which occurs in juveniles though these lack blaze. HABITS: Much as 134; most British birds occur in large flocks of 137. MAY BE CONFUSED with 134, 135, 136, and especially 137.

139 Canada Goose, *Branta canadensis.* Introduced resident, now widespread England; scarcer Wales, Scotland (to Perthshire), N. Ireland. Usually near a lake or pond, sometimes by rivers. DESCRIPTION: 30-40 inches (body 21-24). Sexes alike. Body colour and head pattern distinguishes it from 140 and 141. Juveniles practically as adults. VOICE: Trumpeting *oink* call. HABITS: Nests in single pairs or small groups and flocks form in winter. General habits much as 'grey' geese; grazes on grassland near lakes. In flightless period of late summer runs well if chased. MAY BE CONFUSED with 140, 141.

140 Barnacle Goose, *Branta leucopsis.* Winter visitor; widespread but very local, mainly Hebrides, south-west Scotland, north and west Ireland. Grassland near shore. DESCRIPTION: 23-27 inches (body 17-18). Sexes alike. Juveniles duller, more barred. VOICE: Usual call resembles barking of small dogs rather than honk of grey geese. HABITS: Much as other geese, but rather less suspicious of human approach. Usually on land but occasionally seen on water. MAY BE CONFUSED with 139, 141.

141 Brent Goose, *Branta bernicla.* Very local winter visitor in two distinct races; dark-breasted race mainly down east coast from R. Tay; pale-breasted race in north and west Scotland, Hebrides, Ireland. Tidal areas: estuaries, bays, and islands. DESCRIPTION: 22-24 inches (body 16-17). Sexes alike. Smallest and squattest of commoner geese. Dark race (not shown) has upper and underparts much the same shade of grey. White mark on side of neck absent in juvenile. VOICE: Usual call resembles croak, rather than bark or honk. HABITS: Spends more time on water than other geese, feeding on sea-grass, *Zostera*. Flock may be seen as black patch far out on tidal mud. Flocks fly in packs more like 156 than other geese. MAY BE CONFUSED with 139, 140, and in flight with 156, 157.

142 Shelduck, *Tadorna tadorna.* Resident, partly migrating to moult; widespread round coasts, occasionally inland. Estuaries and coasts with sand-dunes, marshes, or heaths; occasionally along rivers inland. DESCRIPTION: 24 inches (body 16). Sexes almost alike. Big, upstanding duck with piebald appearance at a distance. Speculum chestnut and glossy green. Juveniles have dull brown upper parts and lack collar. VOICE: Repeated barking quack is usual call, more likely to be confused with calls of divers (175–7) than with other ducks. HABITS: Sometimes on water but usually walking about muddy shores or marshland in pairs within a larger social unit. Slow beating flight more like geese than other ducks but black-and-white pattern distinctive. MAY BE CONFUSED with 158 drake.

143 Mallard, *Anas platyrhynchos.* Resident; winter visitor and passage migrant; neighbourhood of fresh water of all types, also estuaries and sea-lochs. DESCRIPTION: 23 inches (body 15). Sexes differ, but both have grey wings with deep purple-blue speculum bordered white above and below. Drake in eclipse much as duck. Legs orange. See also p. 221. VOICE: Loud repeated quack, reminiscent of farmyard ducks, is usual call of duck; drake is quieter but higher-pitched. HABITS: Spends much time on water or on its edge, perching in branches as well as sitting on banks. Feeds in water by upending like farmyard ducks; on land walks swiftly with horizontal posture. Has fast-beating flight action typical of ducks and audible at a distance; flies by moonlight inland to feed on fields. Pairs scatter to breed but form flocks in autumn. MAY BE CONFUSED (drake) with 149, 152, 158, 159; (duck) with 144, 148, 149.

144 Gadwall, *Anas strepera.* Local resident (partly introduced) Scilly, E. Anglia, Somerset, London area, Forth and Tay areas, elsewhere in Scotland; winter visitor more widely but scarce. Freshwater lakes, lochs, slow-running rivers, and marshes. DESCRIPTION: 20 inches (body 13). Sexes differ. Duck, much like 143 but greyer and more mottled looking; at rest bright orange lines down side of dull bill are a good point. Speculum distinctive: red, black, and white. Drake in eclipse much as duck. Legs orange. See also p. 221. VOICE: Duck's quack much like 143 but quieter; drake's more of a croak. HABITS: Much as 143 with which odd birds or pairs often found. MAY BE CONFUSED with ducks of 143, 148, 149.

145 Wigeon, *Anas penelope.* Local resident, Scotland, very local indeed in England; general in winter. Breeds usually on small sheets of fresh water; in winter on lakes, reservoirs, floodwater, estuaries. DESCRIPTION: 18 inches (body 12). Sexes differ. Duck more richly coloured than 143 with dark chestnut head and lighter chestnut flanks. Wings greyish with narrow white bars round dull green speculum. White underparts prominent in flight; see also p. 221. Rounded forehead distinguishes both sexes from other similar species. VOICE: Drake's *whee-oo* whistle is distinctive. HABITS: In general as 143, but does not perch off ground and often grazes along banks of lakes etc.; also feeds much in estuaries. Large flocks build up in favoured waters. Faster wing-beats than 143 and looks smaller, thinner-winged, with more compact body. MAY BE CONFUSED with 146.

146 Teal, *Anas crecca.* Resident, passage migrant and winter visitor; more on marshes and shallow water areas than 143 and less on tidal water. DESCRIPTION: 14 inches. Sexes differ. Duck a grey-brown bird, mottled black with no stripe over eye. Black and green speculum with white inner border. Legs greyish. See also p. 221. VOICE: Drake has repeated granular *shrit* call; duck usually silent. HABITS: Feeds much on wet ground where busy, fast-running birds look like flock of waders; also very quick in flight manoeuvres. Sometimes rests on water. MAY BE CONFUSED with 145, 147.

147 Garganey, *Anas querquedula.* Scarce summer visitor to east and south-east England; occasional in many other areas. Much as 146, but not on bogs. DESCRIPTION: 15 inches. Sexes differ. Broad grey-blue area on wing distinctive in all plumages; green speculum bordered with white. Duck much as 146 but has dull brownish-green speculum, paler wing, faint stripe over eye, and pale throat. In general, if 146 is miniature 143 in shape, Garganey is more like 149, even to rather longer and flatter bill. See also p. 221. VOICE: Rather silent, except for drake's grating call in spring. HABITS: More like 149 than 146 and seldom in numbers: usually only a pair. MAY BE CONFUSED with 146.

148 Pintail, *Anas acuta.* Local resident, breeding east and south-east-England, sporadic in Scotland, rarely Ireland; widespread in winter becoming very common locally in estuaries. Usually near lakes for nesting. DESCRIPTION: 22 inches (body 14). Sexes differ. A big duck, more elongated than 143. Duck much lighter than 143 and has noticeably pointed tail. Speculum greeny-brown, but duller in female, with buff margin which gives pale edge to wing in flight. Legs greyish. See also p. 221. VOICE: Rarely heard; duck has a low-pitched quack. HABITS: Feeds on banks of fresh water lakes and marshes, and on estuaries like 145, both in water or walking and running. Fast wing action with distinctive silhouette make it easy to recognize in flight. Carries neck stretched when swimming and slightly alarmed. MAY BE CONFUSED (duck) with 143, 144, 149.

149 Shoveler, *Anas clypeata.* Resident, widespread, but rare or very local Scottish Highlands; winter visitor and passage migrant. Shallow fresh water and estuaries, marshes. DESCRIPTION: 20 inches (body 12). Sexes differ. Duck much as 143 but dumpier build and long spatulate bill distinguish her. Forewing pale blue; speculum green bordered white. See also p. 221. VOICE: Generally silent; duck quacks. HABITS: Characteristic shovelling method of feeding on surface of water. In flight rather like 145, but shape distinct. Seldom moves about on land. MAY BE CONFUSED with 143, duck with 144, 148.

150 Pochard, *Aythya ferina.* Local resident down east side Britain, very local on west and only occasional Ireland; widespread in winter. Rather large freshwater lakes, reservoirs, and ponds. DESCRIPTION: 18 inches (body 12). Sexes differ. Pochard and 151-3 are much rounder and dumpier than 143-9. Wings dark with no obvious speculum. Forehead noticeably sloping. Legs grey. See also p. 221. VOICE: Duck utters low growl in breeding season. HABITS: A diving duck, unlike 143-9, which only dive exceptionally; swims with tail low on water. Whole party often dives almost together. Does not take flight readily and flies with rapid beats after heavy take off. MAY BE CONFUSED with rare Red-crested Pochard *Netta rufina.*

151 Tufted Duck, *Aythya fuligula.* Resident; widespread in breeding season, general in winter. Habitat much as 150. DESCRIPTION: 17 inches (body 11). Sexes differ. In shape much as 150 but head tufted, not smoothly rounded. Some ducks show white area under tail. Legs greyish. See also page 221. VOICE:

as 150. HABITS: Much as 150 but flies more readily; on the other hand becomes very tame in winter, e.g. on London ponds where fed. MAY BE CONFUSED with 152, 153, and with rare Ferruginous Duck *Aythya nyroca*.

152 **Scaup,** *Aythya marila*. Winter visitor and passage migrant, breeding sporadically, perhaps regularly Scotland. Mainly estuaries and bays; inland on lakes and reservoirs. DESCRIPTION: 19 inches (body 12½). Sexes differ. Vermiculated grey back distinguishes drake from 151. Duck very like 151 but has obvious white blaze all round bill though many Tufted Ducks have some white at base of bill. Both sexes have white wing-bar a little wider than 151. See p. 221. Legs dull blue-grey. HABITS: A sea-duck and therefore often difficult to see clearly. Feeds by diving in quite deep water. Social in winter and flocks often seen out to sea flying in rather ragged formation. MAY BE CONFUSED with 151, drake with 153.

153 **Goldeneye,** *Bucephala clangula*. Winter visitor and passage migrant, on lakes, reservoirs, and pools of all sizes, large rivers, estuaries, and bays. Bred Inverness-shire, 1970-1. DESCRIPTION: Drake 18 inches (body 12); duck smaller. Sexes differ. Big head and short thick bill distinctive. Young drakes resemble ducks. Both sexes have parallel broad white wing-bars, see p. 221. HABITS: Appears longer and lower in water than 150-2. When in flight, fast-beating wings audible at a distance. Odd birds or small parties usually keep to themselves. MAY BE CONFUSED with 151, 152, 158.

154 **Long-tailed Duck,** *Clangula hyemalis*. Winter visitor on open sea, mainly north Scotland and east coast; rare inland; has bred. DESCRIPTION: 17 inches (body 11½) without tail feathers of male. Sexes differ. A rather small, round duck, with long, pointed tail. In summer (not shown) upper parts of drake become much darker, with only whitish patches on head. Wings dark in both sexes, see p.222. Legs greyish. VOICE: Drake utters musical yodelling call, which is characteristic of flocks out on the water. HABITS: Very much a sea duck, swimming buoyantly; drakes may elevate or trail their long tail streamers. Flies over water with turning action almost like a wader, and wings kept very low. Like other sea ducks, flocks fly in irregular formations.

155 **Eider,** *Somateria mollissima.* Resident round most of Scottish coast and into Northumberland, north-west England and Ireland as far as Sligo; non-breeding birds much farther south. Sea-coasts and islands. DESCRIPTION: 23 inches (body 15). Sexes differ. Duck has variable brownish speculum, bordered whitish. Heavy body and long-nosed 'Norman' profile characteristic of this species and can be confused only with very rare King Eider, but there are many baffling plumages of young males with white breasts, etc., and drakes in eclipse retain white on wings and have pale tops to their heads. See also p. 221. VOICE: Crooning of drakes characteristic of spring gatherings and can be heard a long way away. HABITS: A sea duck, breeding usually socially and remaining in parties throughout the year, though odd birds often seen. Lands on beaches, waddling heavily like domestic duck and sits on rocks. Flies low and powerfully, usually in line. MAY BE CONFUSED (duck) with 156, 157.

156 **Common Scoter,** *Melanitta nigra.* Rare resident, breeding north Scotland and west Ireland, but may be seen round coasts, especially east side Britain, all through year; occasional inland. Breeds fresh-water lochs; otherwise offshore but not on very rocky coasts. DESCRIPTION: 19 inches (body 12½). Sexes differ. Duck has conspicuous pale patch on cheek. Young males in plumages between drake and duck are rather perplexing. Legs blackish. See also p. 222. VOICE: Drake has variously described piping call, often uttered in concert. HABITS: Usually seen as raft of dark birds out to sea, or flying low over water in irregular lines. Seldom comes in close unless oiled or injured, and occasionally lands, when very clumsy. Mass diving common. MAY BE CONFUSED with 141, 155 (duck), 157, and with very rare Surf Scoter, *Melanitta perspicillata.*

157 **Velvet Scoter,** *Melanitta fusca.* Winter visitor and passage migrant, mainly down east and south-east coasts; local in west. Habitat as 157, but rare inland. DESCRIPTION: 22 inches (body 14). All plumages distinguished from 156 by white wing-bar when visible. Ducks and immature birds like 156, but with two distinct pale patches on face. See also p. 222. HABITS: Much as 156 but considered to be less shy and does not form large flocks. MAY BE CONFUSED with 141 (in flight), 156.

158 **Goosander,** *Mergus merganser.* Resident most of Scotland and

extreme north England; in winter widespread but local. Breeds wooded lochs and rivers, even quite small burns; in winter on rivers, estuaries, lakes, and reservoirs. DESCRIPTION: Drake 26 inches (body 18); duck smaller. Sexes differ. 'Cigar' shape distinguishes drakes from 143, 153; breast looks white in distance. Duck has rough, almost crested crown. Immature drakes much as duck. Legs red. See also p. 222. HABITS: Swims low in water and usually seen in small parties well away from shore. Quite agile on shore in breeding season when pairs may be seen on rivers. Cigar-shaped body in flight low over water. MAY BE CONFUSED with 159, (drakes) with 143, 153; (ducks) with 170; in flight with 170, 177.

159 **Red-breasted Merganser,** *Mergus serrator.* Resident north and south-west Scotland, Ireland, north-west England, North Wales. Widespread in winter. Breeds all types freshwater, estuaries, and sheltered coasts; in winter round coasts, seldom inland. DESCRIPTION: 23 inches (body 14). Sexes differ. Drake superficially like 143, but cigar body and snaky head distinguish. Duck much as 158, but sides darker, general tint browner; head relatively thinner, crest more wispy; throat patch not pure white. Immature drakes much as duck. See also p. 222. VOICE: Duck quacks when alarmed. HABITS: Swims low and flies low with rather squattering action; white bars show up prominently. Feeds close in, diving smoothly. In winter in small parties, but in late summer many brown-headed birds gather near breeding area. MAY BE CONFUSED with 158; (drake) with 143, 149; (duck) with 160, 170.

160 **Smew,** *Mergus albellus.* Winter visitor, widespread but local, commonest in south. Sheets of freshwater, often quite small; sometimes very sheltered coasts. DESCRIPTION: Drake 16 inches (body 10); duck smaller. Immature drakes resemble duck. See also p. 222. HABITS: Usually seen in small parties well out on water; habits much as 158, 159. Adult drakes rather scarce. MAY BE CONFUSED (duck) with 159, 171-4.

PELICAN ORDER

Very large sea-birds. Sexes alike. Social during breeding season. Dive expertly, either from air or from surface.

161 Gannet, *Sula bassana.* Colonies chiefly west side British Isles, on oceanic islands, occasionally cliffs. DESCRIPTION: 36 inches (body 23).Sexes alike. Juveniles dark brown with white spots; immature birds gradually become whiter. VOICE: Silent, except in breeding colonies. HABITS: Flies with neck stretched and series of fast beats with alternating glides, looking mechanical when compared with gulls. Vertical or sloping dives send up plume of spray. Often in small parties, with adults and immatures mixed. Swims buoyantly but does not come ashore unless injured or oiled. Breeds in large, closely-packed colonies. MAY BE CONFUSED with big gulls 228–32, immatures with 162, 163, 167, 175–7.

162 Cormorant, *Phalacrocorax carbo.* Resident and summer visitor, widespread but local. Breeds cliffs and rocky islands around coasts, locally on freshwater lochs, inland cliffs; in winter on rivers and reservoirs. DESCRIPTION: 36 inches (body 22). Sexes alike. Hoary appearance on head and white flank patches (as shown) only in spring. Juveniles brown with lighter underparts and throat; immatures resemble adults but with extensive white area on underparts. VOICE: Silent except in breeding colonies. HABITS: Usually seen flying low over water with slower beats of broader wings than 161. Swims low in water, often only head and neck showing, and dives from surface. Spends much time in bottle-like stance on rocks, or with wings stretched in heraldic posture. Much more often inland than 163 and perches on trees. Breeds often in closely packed colonies. MAY BE CONFUSED with 163, 175–7 and with immature 161.

163 Shag, *Phalacrocorax aristotelis.* Resident, breeds sea-cliffs, caves, and screes; in winter round rocky coasts; occasional inland waters after storms. DESCRIPTION: 30 inches (body 18). Sexes alike. Adults distinctly smaller than 162; prominent tufted crest (as shown) for short period in spring. Head rounder, less ruffled than 162. Brown juveniles very difficult to tell apart though bills always thinner. VOICE: Silent except at breeding sites. HABITS: Much as 162, but often jumps clean out of water before diving. Perches regularly on rocks in numbers, but not so much on smooth shores. Breeds colonially but more scattered than 162. MAY BE CONFUSED with immature 161, 162, 175–7.

SHEARWATER AND PETREL ORDER

Small to large sea-birds, only coming on land to breed or when storm-driven. Sexes alike. Larger species glide long distances with short bursts of flapping. Feed by diving, scavenging, and picking off water. Often social throughout the year.

164 **Storm Petrel,** *Hydrobates pelagicus.* Resident and summer visitor to west coasts of Britain and Ireland, Orkney and Shetland. Breeds rocky oceanic islands, occasionally mainland headlands; in winter on open sea, though occasionally blown inland in numbers. DESCRIPTION: 6 inches. Sexes alike. A very small sooty-black sea-bird with white rump and square-cut tail. VOICE: Whickering call in dark over nesting places, in which continuous purr is uttered. HABITS: When seen in daylight out to sea flies just above water with trailing legs, fluttering and gliding alternately. Only comes to nesting holes by night. MAY BE CONFUSED with 165 and other rarer petrels.

165 **Leach's Petrel,** *Oceanodroma leucorrhoa.* Rare resident and summer visitor, very local in Hebrides; has bred Irish islets. Wind-blown inland. Habitat as 164. DESCRIPTION: 8 inches. Sexes alike. Bigger and browner than 164, but dark feathers in centre of rump and slightly forked tail are not easy to see in field. VOICE: Complicated whickering call on wing over nesting place also used in nest-holes and quite distinct from 164. HABITS: Flight distinct from 164, much more agile and with frequent changes of direction. Nocturnal at nesting place. MAY BE CONFUSED with 164 and rarer petrels.

166 **Manx Shearwater,** *Puffinus puffinus.* Resident and summer visitor, western and northern islands of Britain and Ireland; non-breeders more widespread. Breeds oceanic islands, usually with plenty of turf, occasionally rocky hilltops and on headlands; off-shore waters for feeding. DESCRIPTION:

14 inches. Sexes alike. Black above and white below in striking contrast; relatively long, thin wings. VOICE: Remarkable crowing noises uttered over and in nesting burrows at night. HABITS: Usually seen flying in parties low over water appearing to 'shear water' with each wing in turn; also in huge flocks or rafts on water. Nocturnal to nesting places. Breeds in large colonies. MAY BE CONFUSED with 167, 168, and in flight with 238, 239.

167 **Great Shearwater,** *Puffinus gravis*. Non-breeding summer visitor, mainly off western coasts. DESCRIPTION: 17–18 inches. Sexes alike. Bigger than 166 and much lighter-coloured above with distinct darker cap and white of throat extending round neck. In flight white patch shows at base of tail. HABITS: Most likely to be seen out to sea, gliding over waves for long distances with occasional series of wing-beats. Lands on water briefly to feed. Solitary or several close together. MAY BE CONFUSED with immature 161, 166, 168.

168 **Sooty Shearwater,** *Puffinus griseus*. Autumn visitor, mainly off western coasts. DESCRIPTION: 16 inches. Sexes alike. Size much as 167, but dark sooty brown all over with pale line under wing. HABITS: Much as 167 with which often seen. MAY BE CONFUSED with 167 and rarer shearwaters, 234–7.

169 **Fulmar,** *Fulmarus glacialis*. Resident and summer visitor, widespread but local round British coasts. Breeds cliffs, steep banks, buildings, even flat ground and inland crags and quarries; at large over sea. DESCRIPTION: 18½ inches. Sexes alike. General colouring like a gull, but has short neck, heavy head and stout-looking bill due to external nostrils. Mantle and wings often look brown rather than grey and there is rare phase dark all over. VOICE: Croaking note on water and distinctive cackle at breeding places between pairs or groups of birds. HABITS: Holds wings stiffly in flight and glides with short bursts of wing-beats quite unlike any gull; fond of coasting along cliff-tops. Continual coming and going from breeding places which may form large but scattered colonies. Lands on water to feed. MAY BE CONFUSED with 227, 228, 231, 232.

GREBE ORDER

Medium to large water-birds with straight bills and lobed toes. Sexes
alike. Bright plumages in summer. Clumsy on land, feed by diving.
Reluctant to fly, when they look like thin ducks with feet splayed.

170 Great Crested Grebe, *Podiceps cristatus.* Widespread resident
except highland areas. Breeds inland waters usually with
reed and other cover; occasionally on slow-flowing rivers
but not on small ponds. In winter shifts to coasts, estuaries,
open lakes, and reservoirs. DESCRIPTION: 19 inches (body 12).
Sexes alike. A long-necked, sharp-billed water-bird with remarkable head adornments in summer. White wingbar shows
conspicuously in flight. In winter only traces of head-dress
remain and whole cheek area looks white. Juveniles resemble
winter plumage with striped heads. Legs mainly green, toes
lobed. VOICE: Variety of notes during courtship and breeding:
a loud bark, a double-note uttered from cover; *kee-wick* like
hunting call of Tawny Owl. The shrill calls of young begging
for food are penetrating. HABITS: Swims gracefully, rather low
in water with neck up and bill slightly downward. Complicated
displays in spring and rapid charges over water at rivals. Feeds
by diving. In flight looks very thin and elongated, with neck
stretched slightly downward and feet splayed out. MAY BE
CONFUSED with females of 158, 159, with 171, and with
juveniles of 247.

171 Red-necked Grebe, *Podiceps griseigena.* Scarce winter visitor,
mainly east side Britain. Estuaries and sheltered shores; rather
rarer inland on reservoirs and lakes. DESCRIPTION: 17 inches
(body 10). Sexes alike. Usually seen in winter plumage in
Britain and resembles 170 but is smaller, more compact, shorter
necked; also dark cap descends right to eye and neck is usually
darker while relatively thick bill and big head make it look
rather top heavy. Summer plumage distinctive with red neck,
white cheeks, and dark crown with ear-tufts. HABITS: As
170 in winter. MAY BE CONFUSED in winter with 170, 172, 173,
238–41.

172 Slavonian Grebe, *Podiceps auritus.* Rare resident; breeds very
locally north Scottish Highlands. Widespread in winter. Breeds
small lochs with sedge beds; in winter on estuaries, sea-lochs,

and sheltered bays, sometimes on reservoirs and lakes. DES-CRIPTION: 13 inches (body 8). Sexes alike. A small grebe with straight pick-axe bill and white wing patch. In winter becomes dark above and white below, but dark crown stops at eye-level and white areas of cheeks extend to nape of neck (see 173). First winter birds are darker. VOICE: Silent in winter but has variety of calls in breeding season of which prolonged whin-nying is most common; young have shrill food-begging call like 170. HABITS: A round-bodied bird on water with relatively long, thin neck, feeding by frequent dives with upward jump. Flies with rapid wing-beats, showing white wing-patch. Social in breeding season, but usually solitary in winter. MAY BE CONFUSED in winter with 170, 171, 173, 174, 238–241.

173 **Black-necked Grebe,** *Podiceps nigricollis.* Rare resident; breeds sporadically several areas, most regularly east Scotland. In winter mainly on east side and English Midlands. Breeds smallish freshwater sheets with good cover; in winter much as 172 but more often inland. DESCRIPTION: 12 inches (body 7). Sexes alike. Resembles 172 in summer but has black neck and tuft on head golden rather than yellow, also larger white wing-patch; but upturned bill best characteristic in all plumages and can be recognized at quite long range. In winter very like 172, but dark area of crown usually extends well below eye. VOICE: Generally rather silent, but has two soft call-notes and a whinnying call less noisy than 172. HABITS: Much as 172 at all times, though more retiring in breeding season, perhaps owing to thicker cover of breeding waters. MAY BE CONFUSED with 171, 172, 174, 238–241.

174 **Little Grebe,** *Tachybaptus ruficollis.* Resident and winter vis-itor, local north Scotland. Fresh waters of all kinds, usually with thick cover; in winter on estuaries, bays, and open reservoirs. DESCRIPTION: 10½ inches (body 6). Sexes alike. Much smaller, rounder and darker than other grebes in all plumages; very reduced pale wing-bar. Dullish brown all over in winter, paler underneath but never clear white like 172, 173. VOICE: Whinny, heard mostly in breeding season, is characteristic but varies in duration and pitch; also soft double alarm note. HABITS: Swims buoyantly, or can depress itself in water like other grebes; flies with rapid beats and splayed feet. Can land and walk quite well. Very retiring in breeding season, but often

in parties on open waters in winter. MAY BE CONFUSED with 172, 173, and with young of 246, 247.

DIVER ORDER

Large water-birds with long straight bills and partly webbed feet. Sexes alike. Plumage and habits much as grebes, but fly more freely with necks stretched and head held below line of body, giving sinuous, slightly hump-backed appearance.

175 **Great Northern Diver,** *Gavia immer.* Winter visitor, especially Scotland, where bred 1970. Generally sheltered coastal waters; sometimes large sheets of fresh water, especially when injured or oiled. DESCRIPTION: 27-32 inches (body 17-20). Sexes alike. A very large water bird with streamlined body, stout neck, and powerfull bill. In winter loses all adornments, becomes dark brown above and white below, from throat downwards. Very hard to distinguish from 176. VOICE: Generally silent in Britain, but has eerie wail, famous in America as call of the 'loon' and a repeated barking quack on wing. HABITS: Usually seen offshore swimming low in water and diving from time to time. MAY BE CONFUSED with immature 161, 162, and with 176, 177.

176 **Black-throated Diver,** *Gavia arctica.* Rare resident, breeds north Scotland, Hebrides; in winter rare round coasts and occasional inland. Breeds larger lochs; in winter much as 175. DESCRIPTION: 22–27 inches (body 14–17). Sexes alike. In winter very like 175 but upper parts darker and more uniform; this is not so of juveniles where best distinguishing feature may be thinner bill. VOICE: Barking quacks on wing much as 177, also the 'loon' wail. HABITS: Swims and flies much as 175. Usually lands only at nest-site. Solitary when breeding but small parties may form in autumn. MAY BE CONFUSED with immature 161, 162, and with 175, 177.

177 **Red-throated Diver,** *Gavia stellata.* Resident, breeds north Scotland and Islands, one area west Ireland; widespread in winter. Breeds small lochs in moorland; in winter much as 175. DESCRIPTION: 21–23 inches (body 14–15). Smallest of divers, distinguished in all plumages by tip-tilted bill. In winter neck and cheeks white, crown and nape uniform grey-brown and back mottled with white; immatures darker. VOICE:

Barking quack and 'loon' wail as 176, also bedlam of growls and cries connected with courtship and display. HABITS: As other divers, but flies more readily. MAY BE CONFUSED with immature 161, 162, and with 175, 176.

PIGEON ORDER

Medium to large full-bodied land-birds with short, puffy bills and red legs. Sexes alike. Song a form of coo or purr. Wings sharply angled in powerful flapping flight. Feed largely on grain and seeds. Social outside breeding season.

178 **Woodpigeon,** *Columba palumbus.* Resident in woodlands, especially conifer belts, and all types of wooded country, including urban parks and city streets. DESCRIPTION: 16 inches. Sexes alike. Biggest and bulkiest pigeon. Juveniles have no white collar. VOICE: Coo now analysed as *Two coos Taffy take* and usually repeated several times. HABITS: Takes off noisily into powerful flapping flight with wings strongly angled; approaching head on may be mistaken for quite dissimilar birds, e.g. hawks or waders. Many pairs may nest near together and huge flocks form in autumn, swarming over trees before landing on ground. MAY BE CONFUSED with 179, 180.

179 **Stock Dove,** *Columba oenas.* Resident England, Wales, south Scotland but becoming local to absent in north. Becomes scarce to absent westward across Ireland. Wooded farmland, also neighbourhood of ruins, cliffs, and sand-dunes; sometimes in towns. DESCRIPTION: 13 inches. General plumage much as 178, but no white on neck or wings, which have two narrow black bars. No white on underside of tail. VOICE: Rather hoarse repeated *oo-hoo* or *oo-hoo-woo* quite unlike coo of 178. HABITS: Much less noisy than 178, but general actions similar. Forms flocks but seldom of great size; roosts in trees. MAY BE CONFUSED with 178 (especially juveniles), 180.

180 **Rock Dove,** *Columba livia.* Resident, west coasts of Scotland and Ireland and islands; elsewhere stock submerged by escaped domestic pigeons. Inhabits sea cliffs and caves, feeding on fields, cliff-tops, and shore. DESCRIPTION: 13 inches. Sexes alike. General resemblance to 179, but upperparts paler blue-grey, breast grey without pink tinge, two

prominent black bars on wing and extensive white rump. Juveniles duller. VOICE: Coos like domestic pigeon of which it is ancestor. HABITS: Usually seen in fast flight of typical racing pigeon. Social at all times, feeding in small flocks on fields some way inland. MAY BE CONFUSED with 178, 179 and very hard to tell from some racing pigeons.

181 **Turtle Dove,** *Streptopelia turtur.* Summer visitor (end April), general to widespread England and Wales; breeds south-east Scotland; has bred east Ireland, otherwise rare visitor. Farmland with tall hedges, bushy commons and small thickets, large gardens and orchards. DESCRIPTION: 11 inches. Sexes alike. Long fan-tail black, prominently edged white; small patch of alternate black and white streaks on neck, absent in juvenile. VOICE: Vibrant, crooning purr usually in groups of three and quite distinctive. HABITS: Often seen flying up from dusting or swallowing grit on road when black and white tail takes the eye. Angled wing very marked in veering flight. Usually seen in pairs soon after arrival, but flocks form in summer for feeding and may be seen strung out on wires above fields. MAY BE CONFUSED with 112, 256.

See also 256, p. 220.

WADER-GULL-AUK ORDER

The next largest order to the Passerines, as far as British birds are concerned; has three distinct groups, usually regarded as separate sub-orders.

Wader sub-order: numerous and variable group of long-legged, predominantly long-billed birds feeding along shores by wading in shallow water. Sexes usually alike. Divided into several groups of which **plovers** (207-13) have short bills. Wings usually sharply pointed and strongly angled in fast beating flight, though some species have spasmodic, jerky action. Many species social outside breeding season and perform remarkable flight evolutions, turning and twisting in rippling unison, showing now white, now dark.

182 **Black-tailed Godwit,** *Limosa limosa.* Winter visitor and passage migrant; breeds East Anglia, sporadically elsewhere.

Mainly estuaries and big bays; less commonly inland on marshes, reservoirs, and sewage farms. DESCRIPTION: 15-17 inches (bill may be 5). Sexes alike. A big wader with long legs and long slightly upturned bill. In winter (not shown) upperparts grey-brown, including faintly barred breast; much paler underparts; in flight broad white bar along rather dark wing and black and white tail distinctive; but tail often difficult to see at rest. VOICE: Rather silent except on breeding ground, when call is *kee vit*, but flocks have triple call in flight. HABITS: From single birds to flocks of hundreds in favoured localities. Usually looks bigger than 183 but there is much size variation; in flight feet project some way beyond tail. Walks rather slowly and wades up to breast, dipping head to feed. MAY BE CONFUSED with 183, 184, 185, 204, 206, 216.

183 **Bar-tailed Godwit,** *Limosa lapponica.* Winter visitor and passage migrant to estuaries, bays, and mud-flats; occasionally inland. DESCRIPTION: 14-15 inches (bill may be 4). Sexes alike. Rather smaller as a rule than 182 and with more upturned bill, but in winter (not shown) very similar with lighter, greyer upperparts. Easily distinguished in flight as wings uniform grey and tail barred grey below whitish rump. VOICE: Flocks have a barking call in flight. HABITS: Faster mover than 182, but feeding habits similar. MAY BE CONFUSED with 182, 184, 185, 205, 206.

184 **Curlew,** *Numenius arquata.* Resident, summer and winter visitor, passage migrant, widespread except south-east England. Breeds moorlands, marshes, lowland river valleys, and farmland; in winter all round coasts except very rocky shores. DESCRIPTION: 22–23 inches (bill 5). Sexes alike. The biggest grey-brown wader with long curved bill. No wing-bar; tail barred as 183 with pale rump. VOICE: Liquid *curlee* call unmistakable also shrieking *whaup* of alarm which gives Scottish name. Song beautiful sustained bubbling, rising and falling, and uttered by male in song flight. HABITS: Often seen stalking slowly, pausing to bend neck and probe with long bill; feeds much alone but forms large flocks outside breeding season. Wing-beats rather slower than most waders though faster than gulls. Song flights of male with gliding action and wings held high a feature on breeding ground. MAY BE CONFUSED with 182, 183, 185, immatures of 228–30.

185 **Whimbrel**, *Numenius phaeopus*. Summer visitor, breeding only northern Scottish isles and occasionally on mainland; widespread on passage. Breeds wet moorland; in passage on seashore, occasionally inland. DESCRIPTION: 15–16 inches (bill 3½). Smaller and darker than 184, with shorter bill and almost black crown, divided by a pale central line. VOICE: Usual call a repeated titter, said to be seven notes. HABITS: Much as 184 though not so wary. Seldom in large flocks on passage and often only single birds. Wing-beat faster than 184. Titter call heard inland at night. MAY BE CONFUSED with 182–4.

186 **Woodcock**, *Scolopax rusticola*. Resident, summer and winter visitor, passage migrant. Breeds mainly in woodland; outside breeding season in many types of cover, often near wet ground. DESCRIPTION: 13½ inches (bill 3). Sexes alike. Much more rounded in outline than most waders with long, rather bulbous bill and big eye set far back in flattened head. VOICE: Usually silent when flushed. Spring 'roding' on wing consists of deep growl and high-pitched *chissick*. HABITS: Flushed from ground, flies off silently, twisting through trees. On spring and summer evenings or early mornings birds appear silhouetted in heavy flapping 'roding' flight, bills held downward. MAY BE CONFUSED with 108–10 when flushed.

187 **Great Snipe**, *Gallinago media*. Rare passage migrant, mainly south-east England. Many types of open ground, but often near water. DESCRIPTION: 11 inches (bill 2½). Sexes alike. Almost indistinguishable from 188, except in flight when areas of white on each side of tail show; also rather larger and darker, especially underneath. Young birds do not show much white on tail. VOICE: May utter croak when flushed. HABITS: More like 186 than 188 in flight; usually alone. MAY BE CONFUSED with 188.

188 **Common Snipe**, *Gallinago gallinago*. Resident, winter visitor and passage migrant. Marshy and boggy areas of many types, but seldom amongst trees. DESCRIPTION: 10½ inches (bill 2½). Sexes alike. Very long-billed, rather rounded wader with no wing-bar but russet tip to shortish tail. VOICE: Rises with hissing *whisk*. In breeding season loud, repeated *chipper chipper chipper*. Famous drumming is non-vocal (made by extended tail-feathers and wings in downward flight) and sounds like bleating of goat. HABITS: When flushed, twists away rapidly but may

be watched stalking about and feeding by probing, also resting with bill tucked into wing. Flies like big butterfly with strongly angled wings, rather than with direct beats of most waders. MAY BE CONFUSED with 187, 189.

189 **Jack Snipe,** *Lymnocryptes minimus.* Winter visitor and passage migrant. Habitat much as 188 but often in runnels amongst dry ground. DESCRIPTION: 7½ inches (bill 1½). Sexes alike. Much smaller than 188, with rounder wings and much shorter bill. Plumage more glossy black above with long pale stripes and crown black bordered by pale stripes. VOICE: Usually silent when flushed, but has call distinct from 188. HABITS: Sits much closer than 188, suddenly rising to flop down abruptly only a few yards off. Sometimes indulges in long flights when differences of bill and wing can be seen. MAY BE CONFUSED with 188.

190 **Grey Phalarope,** *Phalaropus fulicarius.* Passage migrant, mainly southern England. Offshore waters, coming in, usually after bad weather, to bays, estuaries, and occasionally inland waters. DESCRIPTION: 8 inches. Sexes alike but female brighter in summer. Wing in flight mainly black with one pronounced white bar; tail black, rump has black centre bordered white. In rarely seen summer plumage nearly all white, except patch on face, replaced by dull red, crown becomes dark and back brown and buff rather like a snipe. Bill usually shows some yellow. VOICE: Usual call is quiet *zit.* HABITS: Usually seen swimming buoyantly like tiny gull and allows very close approach. Jabs at food with side to side movement of bill and also spins round on water, apparently to disturb prey. MAY BE CONFUSED with 191, 199.

191 **Red-necked Phalarope,** *Phalaropus lobatus.* Rare summer visitor; breeds a few Scottish islands and one locality west Ireland. On passage mainly south-east England. Breeds by boggy lochs; at other times as 190. DESCRIPTION: 6½ inches. Sexes alike but female brighter in summer. Wing and tail pattern much as 190, but wing darker. In winter resembles 190, but back more black and less uniform in pattern, while longer, very thin blackish bill distinguishes at all seasons. VOICE: Usual call resembles 190 but lower-pitched. HABITS: In winter as 190; in summer breeds in small groups, females dominating males. MAY BE CONFUSED with 190, 199.

192 Turnstone, *Arenaria interpres.* Winter visitor and passage migrant, preferring rocky shores with seaweed and stony beaches; rare inland. DESCRIPTION: 9 inches. Sexes alike. A medium-sized wader with rather short legs and bill, upper parts brightly coloured in summer. In flight shows white rump, then black crescent, then white and finally black bands across tail; white shoulder patch and bar on wings. In winter upper parts become much duller and head dark brown. VOICE: Usual call-note along shore is rapid whickering, repeated several times. HABITS: Runs rapidly over rocks and shore with head low, bill searching crannies and sometimes turning stones over. Usually in parties, taking flight together in flash of black and white with characteristic call. MAY BE CONFUSED with 204.

193 Knot, *Calidris canutus.* Winter visitor and passage migrant to sandy and muddy shores and estuaries; occasionally inland. DESCRIPTION: 10 inches. Sexes alike. In winter medium sized, plump, whitish wader with rather short bill. Wings very dark grey with thin white stripe, rump and most of tail white with black crescents, tip very dark grey. In summer (not shown) upper parts darker but suffused with light brown and all under-parts up to face become light chestnut, male rather brighter than female. Juveniles and transitional plumages in autumn show pale brown, almost pink breasts. VOICE: Usual call a low-pitched *knot* which may be origin of name; also musical double call *wit wit.* HABITS: Forms dense flocks in some areas and feeds communally after retreating tide; flocks in flight perform fast evolutions in wonderful unanimity, each movement travelling rapidly from bird to bird so that there is continual flicker from dark backs to white undersides. MAY BE CONFUSED with 194, 199, 211.

194 Dunlin, *Calidris alpina.* Resident, summer and winter visitor, passage migrant, breeding locally Scotland, Ireland, north England and Wales; widespread at other times. Breeds high moorland, bogs, coastal marshes; outside breeding season much as 193, but quite regular inland on marshes, sewage farms and by lakes and reservoirs. DESCRIPTION: 7–7½ inches. Sexes alike. Commonest small wader, variable in size and in length of slightly curved bill. Wings very dark with thin white bar, rump, dark grey, bordered white, and tail black. In winter (not shown) upper parts grey-brown, extending to breast; underparts white, but some birds much more grey than brown above and paler underneath. VOICE: Usual call characteristic *shrit*, like wind whistling through metal, developing in breeding season to sustained reel or trill, often uttered in flight. Alarm note *quot quot* may introduce the reel. HABITS: Feeds by running over shore, often in parties or large flocks, but also in association with other species. Evolutions as 193. Odd birds and breeding pairs may allow close approach. MAY BE CONFUSED with 193, 195, 196, 197, 199.

195 Curlew Sandpiper, *Calidris ferruginea.* Passage migrant, mainly east and south coasts of England. Habitat as 194, quite often inland. DESCRIPTION: 7½ inches. Sexes alike. In winter resembles 194, but rather slimmer and more upstanding with more slender and definitely curved bill; wing pattern as 194, but white rump above terminal dark band of tail is distinctive. Beautiful summer plumage seldom seen: whole underparts from face to belly dull red, back suffused bright brown, wings remain greyish. VOICE: Usual call a softer version of 194. HABITS: As 194, with which often found, but seldom in large numbers. MAY BE CONFUSED with 194, 196, 197, 199.

196 Little Stint, *Calidris minuta.* Passage migrant, mainly east side Britain. Habitat as 194. DESCRIPTION: 6 inches. Sexes alike. A very small wader with short straight bill. Usually seen in Britain in transition between summer (as shown) and winter plumage. Wings dark with thin white stripe; rump and tail black with broad white borders. In winter much greyer above and no band across breast. Autumn juveniles show two pale lines down back. VOICE: Single *whit* sometimes developing into continuous twitter. HABITS: As 194, with which often seen, though more active in movements. MAY BE CONFUSED with 194, 195, 197.

197 Temminck's Stint, *Calidris temminckii.* Scarce passage migrant, mainly south-east England; has bred. Mainly inland at marshes, sewage farms, lakes, and reservoirs. DESCRIPTION: 5½ inches. Sexes alike. In all plumages much greyer than 196. Underparts less strikingly white. Brown shades of upper parts disappear in winter and are not shown by juveniles in autumn. Wing and tail pattern much as 196, but outer tail feathers are white. VOICE: High-pitched tittering call when flushed from ground. HABITS: In general much as 194, but fond of hiding in cover, whence towers into flight like Snipe. MAY BE CONFUSED with 194, 195, 196.

198 **Purple Sandpiper,** *Calidris maritima.* Winter visitor and passage migrant to rocky shores and stony beaches. DESCRIPTION: 8 inches. Sexes alike. A stout, very dark little wader with short white stripe on very dark wing, very dark central streak down rump to tail, which is otherwise white to grey. VOICE: Generally silent, but sometimes utters a quiet double call when taking flight. HABITS: Allows very close approach as it stands on rock-faces, blending well with seaweed. Feeds amongst seaweed on rocks and by searching crevices, often with 192, and making short flights when finally disturbed.

199 **Sanderling,** *Calidris alba.* Winter visitor and passage migrant to sandy shores, occasional on mud and inland. DESCRIPTION: 8 inches. Sexes alike. In winter (not shown) the whitest of the smaller waders, whole underparts from face being white and upper parts light grey except for distinctive black shoulder patch; wing also dark with white bar, rump and tail have dark centre bordered white. In summer all upper parts including head, neck and breast, chestnut brown with darker markings and definite boundary with white belly. Plumage shown is transitional autumn state. VOICE: Double call-note rather similar to several other waders, and becomes a continuous twitter from flocks. HABITS: Most active of the small waders, pattering rapidly along water's edge and allowing close approach; feeds in this zone, following retreating surge. Large flocks are wilder than small parties and take wing fairly readily but are less given to aerial manoeuvres than 194 and 195. MAY BE CONFUSED with 190 and 191 in winter plumage, 194, 195.

200 **Ruff,** *Philomachus pugnax.* Winter visitor and passage migrant, mainly east coast; breeds sporadically East Anglia. Inland marshes, less commonly on estuaries and sheltered shores. DESCRIPTION: Male 11–12, female 8½–10 inches. Sexes differ in size and in spring plumage. Male in spring absolutely unique. Females in spring also variable, some much darker than others. Narrow stripe on dark wings; narrow central streak down rump and tail with broad white borders. Most birds seen in Britain in autumn are juveniles with buff faces, throats, and breasts;

female in winter has darker breast and male retains many dark feathers. Legs extremely variable: green, yellow, orange, even red. HABITS: Very upright stance, continually elongating neck and jerks body when alarmed. Feeds with quick downward darts of head at mud. Small parties or odd birds. MAY BE CONFUSED with 204 and (juveniles) with some American sandpipers.

201 **Common Sandpiper**, *Tringa hypoleucos*. Summer visitor (mid-April) to north and west Britain and Ireland; general on passage. Breeds by fast-flowing streams and rivers, by lakes, lochs, and sheltered coasts; on passage on all types of fresh water and estuaries. DESCRIPTION: 8 inches. Sexes alike. A small wader, dull brown above and white below extending in winter to face. Pronounced white bar along wing and rather long, fanned tail has dark centre, bordered white. VOICE: Spring song repeated agitated *kitty-wipy*, *kitty-wipy* breaking into the call-note *kee wee wee*. HABITS: Runs about close to water or perches on stones with tail up and continual bobbing movement; flight very jerky, often shuttering low over water. Usually seen singly, in pairs or in small parties in places not frequented by other waders. MAY BE CONFUSED with 202, 203.

202 **Wood Sandpiper**, *Tringa glareola*. Passage migrant, mainly east side England, to marshes, sewage farms, lakes, reservoirs and coast; a few breed N. Scotland. DESCRIPTION: 8 inches. Sexes alike. Rather larger than 201 with appearance of thinner neck and rounder head than 203. Wing dark, without bar; white rump shading into fanned and barred tail. Upper parts darker, more uniform in winter. VOICE: Usual call when flushed is rapid, shrill *chiff chiff chiff*. HABITS: Less agitated in movements than 201, but bobs its body when uneasy. Flies up quite high when disturbed, but often settles again nearby. Usually ones, twos, or small parties. MAY BE CONFUSED with 201, 203.

203 **Green Sandpiper**, *Tringa ochropus*. Winter visitor and passage migrant to marshes, sewage farms and banks of lakes, reservoirs, and rivers; has bred. DESCRIPTION: 9 inches. Sexes alike. Rather bigger and longer-winged than 202. Upper parts very dark brown, with less mottling in summer than 202, but general pattern similar; wings look almost black in flight with

no bar. White rump area much more extensive than 202, with only narrow dark terminal band on tail VOICE: Usual call when flushed *tit looet looet* much more musical than 202. HABITS: More exaggerated than 202, often flying up to a considerable height when flushed, and skulking much more in vegetation, but having same general actions. MAY BE CONFUSED with 201, 202.

204 **Common Redshank,** *Tringa totanus.* Resident, summer and winter visitor, passage migrant; breeding marshes, wet grass moors, pasture fields, gravel pits, sand dunes, coastal saltings; at other times along coasts (rarer when very rocky) and estuaries. DESCRIPTION: 11 inches. Sexes alike. A medium sized, long-legged wader, distinctly variable but with general grey-brown appearance, browner in summer, greyer in winter. Wings dark with broad white bar along trailing edges; V-shaped white rump shading into barred tail. VOICE: Very noisy, with shrieking call *tui tui tui* and variants. One musical form is heard as song in spring. HABITS: Very excitable, feeding with rapid walk and bobbing movements of head which change to bobbing action of alarm, then takes wing with loud calls. Legs show beyond tail in flight. Seen from single birds to large flocks. MAY BE CONFUSED with 182, 200, 205, 206.

205 **Spotted or Dusky Redshank,** *Tringa erythropus.* Passage migrant, occasionally wintering, mainly east side Britain, local on west. Marshes, sewage farms, banks of lakes and reservoirs, coastal flats. DESCRIPTION: 12 inches. Sexes alike. Bigger, longer-legged, and longer-billed than 204. No wing-bar; rump white, tail barred. In winter upper parts pale grey, barred paler, but wings remain dark; face whitish, underparts white. Juvenile speckled dark brown. VOICE: Double *choo-it* is distinctive. HABITS: Less excitable, more stately than 204. Often feeds by wading deeply, stabbing with bill from side to side. Single birds to small parties, sometimes with other waders. MAY BE CONFUSED with 183, 204, 206.

206 **Greenshank,** *Tringa nebularia.* Summer visitor, breeding locally north Scotland on wet and rocky moorland, sometimes amongst scattered trees; on passage along coasts and estuaries; inland as 205. DESCRIPTION: 12 inches. Sexes alike. A medium to large wader with long legs and long, very slightly upturned bill. No bar on dark wings; extensive white rump and barred

tail. In winter upper parts look grey and white of underparts stretches up to throat. VOICE: Call a rapid *tew tew tew* easily distinguished with practice from 204. Song, uttered by both sexes, repeated *whit-u whit-u whit-u*. HABITS: More horizontal stance than relatives and jerks body rather than bobs it. Flight much as 204 with legs protruding beyond tail. Feeds as 204. Usually in ones, twos, or small parties on passage with odd birds wintering. Perches freely on stones, trees, fence posts on breeding ground. MAY BE CONFUSED with 182, 183, 204, 205.

207 **Kentish Plover,** *Charadrius alexandrinus*. Now scarce passage migrant, south and east coasts. Formerly bred south coast; still breeds Channel Islands. Sand and shingle shores. DESCRIPTION: 6 inches. Sexes almost alike. Black patch on front of crown absent in female whose other dark patches are brown rather than black. Narrow white bar on dark wing and broad white borders to rump and tail. Juveniles resemble female. Legs blackish. VOICE: Calls a repeated *whit* and a churring note. HABITS: Runs about very fast on sand with head usually up, darting quickly after prey. Flight fast with beats marked though not jerky as 201. In small parties on passage. MAY BE CONFUSED with 208, 209, especially their juveniles.

208 **Ringed Plover,** *Charadrius hiaticula*. Resident, winter visitor, and passage migrant on sand and shingle shores, inland on brecks and river shingle; on passage at sewage farms, gravel pits, banks of lakes and reservoirs. DESCRIPTION: 7½ inches. Sexes alike. A much stouter bird than 207, with broad black band across chest. Wing bar broader than 207, but tail pattern much the same. In winter black bands become brown, and much reduced. Juvenile as winter plumage, sometimes with incomplete breast band, so very like 207. Legs yellow. VOICE: Call pleasant piping *pwee*; song a repeated *kitterwee-oo*; various other notes in breeding season. HABITS: Much as 207. Mixes with other small waders freely and scatters widely over mud when feeding; also in compact flocks. MAY BE CONFUSED with 207, 209.

209 **Little Ringed Plover,** *Charadrius dubius*. Local summer visitor, mainly to gravel pits by east-flowing rivers, reaching Scotland in 1968. DESCRIPTION: 6 inches. Sexes alike. Distinguished from 208 at all times by absence of bar on wing,

also rather smaller and yellow ring round eye more prominent. Juvenile much as 208. Legs pinkish, bill less yellow than 208. VOICE: Call *chew* quite distinct from musical note of 208. HABITS: Much as 208. MAY BE CONFUSED with 207, 208.

210 **Golden Plover,** *Pluvialis apricaria.* Resident, winter visitor and passage migrant; breeds locally north and west Britain, Ireland on moorland and bogs, rough pastures; widespread at other times on pastures, stubbles, less common on shore. DESCRIPTION: 11 inches. Sexes practically alike. A medium sized short-billed wader with upper parts at all times spangled golden and brown. In winter underparts are pale and shade into spotted brown breast. In summer northern race (as shown), seen on passage, becomes very black; British breeding birds are lighter. Juveniles as winter. VOICE: Call on breeding ground a plaintive, piping *pe-ew*. In spring a double note described as song, but also wild *terr-heoo terr-heoo terr-heoo* uttered in flight. Winter flight call a whistling *hu-ee*. HABITS: Walks rather upright, dipping to feed. Very fast flight action of pointed wings. Elusive on breeding ground, running amongst tussocks, then suddenly appearing. Winter flocks often with 213. MAY BE CONFUSED with 211, 212.

211 **Grey Plover,** *Pluvialis squatarola.* Winter visitor and passage migrant, mainly to muddy coasts and estuaries, occasionally inland at sewage farms, by lakes, etc. DESCRIPTION: 11 inches. Sexes alike. Loses black breast in winter and upper parts suffused with brown, but always greyer than 210 and in all plumages black patch under wing distinguishes. VOICE: Flight call modulated whistle in three syllables. HABITS: Movements and flights much as 210, but usually found in small parties on coast. MAY BE CONFUSED with 210.

212 **Dotterel,** *Endromias morinellus.* Rare summer visitor, breeding bare mountain-tops above 3,000 feet, Scottish Highlands, sporadic northern England; occasional on passage on bare ground of many types, usually near coast. DESCRIPTION: 8½ inches. Sexes alike but female brighter. Rather faint white bar on dark wings; white spots on end of dark tail. In winter eyestripe obscured, pattern on breast fades to pale brown; juveniles similar. VOICE: Whistling call-note rendered *wit-e-wee* but rather silent, except on breeding grounds. HABITS:

Movements etc., as other plovers but remarkably unafraid and allows close approach. MAY BE CONFUSED with 210.

213 **Lapwing,** *Vanellus vanellus.* Resident, summer visitor, winter visitor, and passage migrant on all types of bare, open country from sea level to 3,000 feet. DESCRIPTION: 12 inches. Sexes almost alike. Only British wader with rounded wings. In winter upper parts dusted over brown, brownish tint over face and neck but throat white. Juvenile similar but crest very small. VOICE: Usual call gives name of *pee-wit* and develops into spring song, usually uttered in tumbling flight. HABITS: Familiarly seen dotted about pasture fields, running a few steps, bending quickly, then standing upright. Flapping flight has scintillating effect owing to black and white under wings and flocks can be recognized at long range. MAY BE CONFUSED with other large-medium waders when seen from behind in winter plumage.

214 **Black-winged Stilt,** *Himantopus himantopus.* Rare visitor, mainly south and east coasts, but has bred Midlands. Shallow pools in marshes. DESCRIPTION: 15 inches (bill 2½). Sexes differ. Extremely long-legged medium-sized wader with conspicuous black and white plumage. Male in summer has varying amount of black on head. Juveniles also have brownish heads. HABITS: Walks slowly with long steps, neck somewhat bent; wades deeply. In flight legs project at least 6 inches beyond tail. MAY BE CONFUSED with 215.

215 **Avocet,** *Recurvirostra avosetta.* Rare resident, summer visitor and passage migrant; breeds very locally East Anglia by very shallow lagoons with low, bare banks; at other times on muddy shores, mainly in south-west. DESCRIPTION: 17 inches (bill 3). Sexes alike. Large black and white wader with thin upturned bill. VOICE: Usual call *kloo-it* gives Dutch name. HABITS: Walks fast with body held horizontal and neck bent, feeds by skimming surface of water with side to side action of bill. In flight legs extend beyond tail and neck usually bent. MAY BE CONFUSED with 214, 226.

216 **Oystercatcher,** *Haematopus ostralegus.* Resident, winter visitor and passage migrant along shores of sand, shingle, and low rock; in north breeds up rivers on riverside fields and moorland and by lochs. DESCRIPTION: 17 inches. Sexes alike. Another big, black

and white wader, with broad white wing-bar. Non-breeders have narrow white band on throat. VOICE: Usual call excited *kleep kleep kleep*, varied by short *pick* note. Song is prolonged piping of call-note. HABITS: Walks rapidly and feeds by probing or attacking shellfish with powerful bill. Flies with fast rather shallow wing-beats. Forms enormous flocks, some persisting all the year round. MAY BE CONFUSED with 182.

217 Stone Curlew, *Burhinus oedicnemus.* Rare summer visitor to downs, brecks, arable land, and shingle beaches in south-east England. DESCRIPTION: 16 inches. Sexes alike. A large, big-headed, short-billed wader; pale bar on closed wing but in flight black flight-feathers with white spots and two pale bars show up; tail rather rounded with dark and pale bands. VOICE: Usual call *coorlee* superficially like 184 but mournful and wailing in quality, resembling call of Little Owl. HABITS: Largely nocturnal; in day-time walks about furtively with body held horizontally and feet put down very deliberately, suddenly breaking into flight. Pairs breed scattered over suitable habitat but parties form in autumn. MAY BE CONFUSED with 184.

Gull sub-order: three groups of sea-birds, sexes alike and predominantly social, especially in breeding season; many have projection on lower mandible called 'gonys'; **terns** 'sea-swallows' – medium sized extremely graceful summer visitors, with thin pointed wings and forked tails, usually white and grey when adult; feed on small fish and insects round coasts and sometimes inland; some species haunt fresh water; **gulls** – large sea-birds, predominantly white when adult and brown when immature, mainly resident and ranging from tern-like to very powerful and rapacious species, omnivorous in diet; **skuas** – parasitic gulls, robbing other species; usually dark brown and spending lives at sea except for breeding season.

218 Black Tern, *Chlidonias niger.* Passage migrant, mainly to southern half England, breeds sporadically. Sheets of fresh water, usually shallow; marshes and sewage farms; rivers; sometimes on coast. DESCRIPTION: 9½ inches. Sexes alike. In summer (as shown) only common dark tern. In winter (and juvenile plumage) underparts, right up to and above bill, and including broad collar, become white. But dark grey smudge in shoulder area distinguishes from very rare White-winged Black Tern. VOICE: Occasional sharp *kick kick* call on passage. HABITS: A fresh water species, feeding by dipping lightly to surface from buoyant, jinking flight. Perching position as shown; walks rather clumsily owing to short legs. MAY BE CONFUSED (in winter) with 219-24.

219 **Gull-billed Tern,** *Gelochelidon nilotica.* Rare visitor, mainly to south and east England; has bred. Habitat as 218. DESCRIPTION: 14-15 inches. Sexes alike. In winter cap becomes grizzled grey and white. Distinction from other terns, especially 220, is heavy black bill with gonys, longer legs, and generally stouter appearance. HABITS: Flight rather heavy for a tern; feeds like 218 over fresh water, even over fields, picking up food off ground; sometimes walks to feed. MAY BE CONFUSED with 218 (winter), 220 (especially).

220 **Sandwich Tern,** *Sterna sandvicensis.* Widespread but very local summer visitor to sandy and shingle beaches, low rocky islands; in Ireland inland by loughs. DESCRIPTION: 15-17 inches. Sexes alike. Bigger and stouter-looking than other common British terns, with tufted appearance at back of crown. Best distinctions: black legs and long black bill with yellow tip. In winter crown becomes grizzled and forehead white. VOICE: Usual call a grating *kurruck* of great carrying power, often heard over sea long before bird is seen. HABITS: A sea-tern, feeding by shallow dives, and usually nesting in very concentrated colonies. Flight intermediate between that of smaller terns and 226. MAY BE CONFUSED with 218 (in winter), 219 (especially), 221-3.

221 **Roseate Tern,** *Sterna dougallii.* Rare summer visitor, mainly to low rocky islands in sea; sometimes sandy shores. DESCRIPTION: 14-15 inches. Sexes alike. Very long tail-streamers; breast looks dead white. Bill mainly black with red base. In winter forehead becomes white and bill quite black, but body always looks whiter than 222 and 223. Juvenile has black marks on grey back and wings, grizzled crown and paler legs. VOICE: Distinctive hoarse alarm-note rendered *aach aach*. HABITS: Much as 222, though flight even lighter and more graceful and wing-beats rapider. MAY BE CONFUSED with 218 (winter), 219, 220, 222, 223.

222 **Common Tern**, *Sterna hirundo*. Summer visitor to low, rocky islands and shores of sand and shingle; coastal turf; inland by rivers, lochs, occasionally marshes and gravel pits. DESCRIPTION: 13-14 inches. Sexes alike. In summer can be told with certainty from 223 only by colour of bill, bright red with black tip, and by longer legs if seen standing. In winter both species have largely black bills, white foreheads and shorter tail-streamers. Juveniles similar with brown on back. VOICE: Distinctive alarm note is long-drawn *kee-rah* with emphasis on *kee*; usual call a repeated *kick kick kick*. Many other notes described and some common to 223. HABITS: Usually seen in graceful jinking flight, hovering to dive just under surface with very little splash and quickly flying up again. Adults very seldom swim unless injured. Perches conspicuously as shown. Walks clumsily. Usually social and breeds large colonies. MAY BE CONFUSED with 218 (in winter), 219-21, 223 (especially); juveniles with 224.

223 **Arctic Tern**, *Sterna paradisaea*. Summer visitor and passage migrant; very local England and Wales; widespread Scotland and Ireland. Habitat as 222. DESCRIPTION: 14-15 inches. Sexes alike. Almost as 222, but bill in spring blood-red, breast usually darker grey and tail-streamers longer; though only bill colour and shorter legs can be relied on for identification. In winter and when juvenile cannot often be told from 222. VOICE: Alarm note lacks long drawn-out first syllable heard from 222 and is almost single *kaar*. High-pitched call *kee kee* also distinctive, but some notes in common with 222. HABITS: As 222, but in general a more excitable, aggressive bird. MAY BE CONFUSED with 218 (in winter), 219-21, 222 especially; juveniles with 224.

224 **Little Tern**, *Sterna albifrons*. Widespread but local summer visitor to beaches with sand, often mixed with much shingle and sometimes with mud. More general on passage and sometimes inland. DESCRIPTION: 9-10 inches. Sexes alike. Much smaller than other 'white' terns, wing relatively narrower and less pointed. White forehead in summer causes confusion with juveniles of 222, 223. In winter much as 222. VOICE: Usual calls less powerful *kick kick* than 222, becoming *ki-ick* in alarm, and soft buzzing *kirri kirri kirri*. HABITS: Much as 222, but flight noticeably more fluttering and tendency to hover

more. Seldom in large flocks or large colonies. MAY BE CON-
FUSED with juveniles of 222, 223.

225 **Little Gull,** *Larus minutus.* Scarce passage migrant and winter
visitor mainly to east side Britain. Sheltered coasts, estuaries;
inland by lakes, rivers, marshes. DESCRIPTION: 11 inches.
Sexes alike. In summer as shown but not often seen Britain.
No black on wings but underside quite dark grey. In winter
loses almost all black on head. Much of juvenile's upper parts
grey-brown with black bars across wing and tail which persist
in immature plumages. Bill black in winter. VOICE: Call *keck
keck keck* not so loud as 226. HABITS: Graceful flight rather like
tern; feeds much in air or off surface of water. Walks easily.
Sometimes in flocks in Britain, but often solitary. MAY BE
CONFUSED with 226 and with rare Sabine's and Bonaparte's
Gulls.

226 **Black-headed Gull,** *Larus ridibundus.* Resident, summer visitor
and winter visitor, widespread but breeds mainly in west and
north of Britain; more general in winter. Breeds along coasts
on tidal marshes and some sandy shores, inland round pools
and small lakes or lochs with boggy margins, also marshes and
sewage farms. DESCRIPTION: 14–15 inches. Sexes alike.
In summer rather like 225 but has chocolate mask and black
wingtips with white mirrors, while underside of wing is pale
grey. In winter mask lost except for spot behind eye. Juvenile
much browner than 225 and immature birds distinguished by
absence of black bar on wing. VOICE: Usual call, laughing
cackle, or single harsh *karr.* HABITS: Often seen soaring with
slightly bent wings high overhead, e.g. in winter over central
London. Flapping flight much heavier than terns, but intermediate between them and ponderous beats of big gulls. Nowa-
days feeds much by scavenging, fighting with others for offal,
etc. Walks quite easily but with a rolling gait. Swims buoyantly
(as shown) with tail well up. Social at all times. MAY BE CON-
FUSED with 225 and with Mediterranean Gull *Larus melanoce-
phalus,* which has nested Hampshire; in winter with 227.

227 **Common Gull,** *Larus canus.* Resident, breeds north and west
Scotland, west Ireland, rarely in England; widespread on passage and in winter, mainly on grassland. Breeds on islets and
rocky shores of sheltered coasts, also inland on lochs and bogs.
DESCRIPTION: 16 inches. Sexes alike. Typical plumage

pattern of many gulls. In winter some faint brown streaks on head. Juvenile is mixture of dull browns; tail whitish with black band. Immature birds grade from this to adult in about two years. Juvenile legs dull pink and bill blackish. VOICE: Gull calls are rather similar, repeated *kyuck kyuck kyuck*, sharper in this species than in 228. Alarm call over breeding ground *kek kek kek*, staccato but not cackling like 226. HABITS: Generally seen in winter soaring overhead or walking about grassland, especially playing fields in towns, when head and neck look much thicker than in 226. Usually in small flocks. MAY BE CONFUSED with 226 (in winter), 228, 233.

228 **Herring Gull**, *Larus argentatus*. Resident and winter visitor; breeds mainly rocky coastlines, including cliffs and islands, also sand dunes and buildings; in winter on estuaries, harbours and inland on rubbish tips and fields, roosting on lakes and reservoirs. DESCRIPTION: 22 inches. Sexes alike. Plumage much as 227 but much bigger, with pink legs and powerful yellow bill with red gonys. Juveniles as 227, but without black band on tail; very difficult to tell from 229. Adult plumage acquired in about three years. VOICE: Long drawn-out *ky-uck ky-uck ky-uck* is typical gull call of maritime 'sound effects'; also laughing *ha ha ha*, often uttered on wing. HABITS: Commonest scavenging gull round ships in harbour, but does not go far out to sea, being replaced by 229 and 233. Active and rapacious, remaining in flocks all the year and breeding often in huge scattered colonies. MAY BE CONFUSED with 227, 231-3 and 184, 229, 234, when immature.

229 **Lesser Black-backed Gull**, *Larus fuscus*. Resident and summer visitor, breeding mainly west and north Britain and Ireland; widespread on passage, local in winter (including Scandinavian race). Habitat much as 228, but less on cliffs and more commonly inland. In winter Scandinavian birds along east coast harbours and estuaries, residents usually near rubbish tips. DESCRIPTION: 21 inches. Sexes alike. Much same size as 228. Mantle much darker in Scandinavian birds and looks black in flight. Juveniles much as 228, but immature birds tend to show darker back and wings as they grow older. VOICE: Difficult to distinguish from 228 but somewhat deeper. HABITS: Much as 228 but follows ships further out to sea. MAY BE CONFUSED with 184, 230, 228 when immature.

230 **Great Black-backed Gull,** *Larus marinus.* Resident and winter visitor, breeds locally north and west Britain and Ireland. Habitat as 228 and 229. DESCRIPTION: 25–27 inches. Sexes alike. Much bigger than 229 when seen together, otherwise distinguished by deep browny-black of back and wings, whitish legs, very powerful head and bill. Immature plumages much as other big gulls, but underparts and head generally paler in contrast to upper parts. VOICE: Deep, growling *uh uh uh* and single surprised-sounding *aw* are characteristic. HABITS: Much as 228 and 229, though seldom following ships. Wing-beat measurably slower than 229. MAY BE CONFUSED with 184, 228 when immature, 229.

231 **Glaucous Gull,** *Larus hyperboreus.* Winter visitor, mainly to east coast, becoming more frequent in north. Habitat coastal. DESCRIPTION: 27 inches. Sexes alike. No black on wing tips in any plumage. Juveniles more uniformly mottled brown than 228–30; immature birds pale biscuit-brown. VOICE: Resembles 228. HABITS: As other big gulls in winter. MAY BE CONFUSED with 232, and 228, 229 when immature.

232 **Iceland Gull,** *Larus glaucoides.* Scarce but widespread winter visitor to coasts and harbours. DESCRIPTION: 21 inches. Sexes alike. Smaller than 231, but difficult to tell individuals apart as plumage almost identical. Wings, however, relatively much longer, reaching well beyond tail when at rest, their tips meeting; bill not so powerful and adults have red rim to eye, not yellow as 231. VOICE: Resembles 228. HABITS: Longer wings give at least appearance of more graceful flight than other big gulls; otherwise similar. MAY BE CONFUSED with 231 and 228, 229 when immature.

233 **Kittiwake,** *Rissa tridactyla.* Widespread but local resident and winter visitor; breeds sea-cliffs or rocky island stacks, on buildings in several places on east coast. Outside breeding season may occur on shore but spends much of year out to sea. DESCRIPTION: 16 inches. Sexes alike. Plumage much as 227, but neater looking bird with grey of wings and back darker and triangular black tip to wing beyond white; legs black. Juvenile plumage basically as adult but surcharged with black spots on back, black bands on neck, wing, and tail. VOICE: *Kitti-waak* call is best known of several at nest-sites; generally silent at sea. HABITS: Although perching freely on shore, usually seen in flight after

ships or swimming. Flight action faster than 227; feeds by picking off surface or shallow dives. MAY BE CONFUSED with
226 (in winter), 227, 228.

234 **Great Skua,** *Stercorarius skua.* Summer visitor, breeding
Orkney, Shetland, Hebrides, a few N. Scotland on bare,
boggy moorland; otherwise oceanic. DESCRIPTION: 23
inches. Sexes alike. Wings have white patch on flight feathers,
visible underneath. Juveniles less streaked and less white on
wings. VOICE: Quacking and laughing notes on breeding
ground; usually silent elsewhere. HABITS: Parasite, scavenger
and killer, pressing home attacks to drive victim into water,
where it feeds, then washes. Breeds in scattered colonies, but
often alone at other times. MAY BE CONFUSED with immatures
of 228-32, and with 235-7.

235 **Long-tailed Skua.** *Stercorarius longicaudus.* Rare passage
migrant mainly off east coast England. DESCRIPTION:
20 inches (up to 8 tail). Sexes alike. Smallest and most
graceful skua. Central tail-feathers sometimes tremendously
elongated but sometimes not much longer than 237. Immature
birds uniform barred and mottled brown and very like 236
and 237; central tail feathers only protrude slightly. HABITS:
As other skuas, but flight more graceful and tern-like. May be
seen in small parties out to sea. MAY BE CONFUSED with 234,
236, 237.

236 **Pomarine Skua,** *Stercorarius pomarinus.* Scarce winter visitor
and passage migrant, mainly off east and south coasts of
England. DESCRIPTION: 20 inches (up to 3 tail). Sexes alike but
two colour phases: light (as shown; much commoner in Britain)
and dark. Dark phase practically uniform dark brown. Both
phases have pale area on wing. Central tail-feathers, which are
blunt-ended, are somewhat elongated and twisted. Juvenile
and immature birds identical with 235 and 237 except for larger
size. VOICE: Whistling and chattering calls recorded. HABITS:
As other skuas. MAY BE CONFUSED with 234, 235, 237.

237 **Arctic Skua,** *Stercorarius parasiticus.* Summer visitor and
passage migrant, breeding bare, boggy moorland in Orkney,
Shetland, some Hebrides, and extreme north Scotland; widespread at other times, often close to shore. DESCRIPTION:
17-18½ inches (up to 3½ tail). Sexes alike but two colour phases,
of which dark (as shown) is commoner in Britain. Plumage

patterns much as 236, but whitish patches on wings less distinct. Central tail feathers elongated, longer than 236, less than 235. Many intermediate plumages between dark and extreme light occur, and light plumages are barred dark brown in winter. Juvenile and immature birds as 235 and 236. VOICE: Mewing and other cries on breeding ground; otherwise usually silent. HABITS: Rakish outline distinguishes smaller skuas from heavier-looking gulls. This species may land on shore when on passage and walks rather clumsily. MAY BE CONFUSED with 234–6.

Auk sub-order: the penguins of the Northern Hemisphere. Sexes alike, with dense, beautifully waterproofed plumage usually dark above and white below. Oceanic except for rather long breeding season when most form large colonies. Mainly fish-eaters. Flight with rapid beats of short wings.

238 **Razorbill,** *Alca torda.* Resident, widespread breeding colonies, except south-east England, on sea-cliffs and steep screes. In winter off-shore; occasionally storm-driven inland. DESCRIPTION: 16 inches. Sexes alike. Wing bar appears as narrow white edge in flight. In winter (juveniles also) throat and sides of face become white. VOICE: Crowing call on breeding stations. HABITS: Swims buoyantly and dives expertly. On land sits in penguin-like manner, normally moving by shuffling, though can walk. Breeds in scattered colonies and disperses outside breeding season. MAY BE CONFUSED with 166, 239, (juvenile) with 241, 242.

239 **Guillemot,** *Uria aalge.* Resident and winter visitor (two races); widespread colonies on sea-cliffs except south-east England. In winter off-shore, occasionally storm-driven inland or when oiled. DESCRIPTION 16½ inches. Sexes alike. Upper parts of southern race chocolate brown; northern race has back and wings almost as dark as 238. A small proportion have white bridle from bill to eye. Winter and juvenile birds have white area on face and neck indistinctly shading into the brown. VOICE: Crowing chorus and other notes at breeding stations, otherwise usually silent. HABITS: Much as 238, except for close-packed breeding. MAY BE CONFUSED with 166, 238, (juvenile) with 241, 242.

240 **Black Guillemot,** *Cepphus grylle.* Resident, breeding locally

Scotland, Ireland, Man, Cumbria, N. Wales; on rocky islands, screes and cliffs with fissures; outside breeding season in neighbouring waters. DESCRIPTION: $13\frac{1}{2}$ inches. Sexes alike. Uniform dark-brown plumage relieved by broad white wing-bar and red legs. In winter (and juveniles) underparts become white and upper parts mottled white all over, though wing-bar remains clear. VOICE: Thin, wheezing whistle in breeding season. HABITS: Much as other auks, but breeds in small, scattered colonies and often seen alone. MAY BE CONFUSED in winter with 171–3.

241 Little Auk, *Plautus alle.* Winter visitor, mainly east coast Britain but may be blown inland in numbers by gales. DESCRIPTION: 8 inches Sexes alike. Much smaller than other auks with very small bill, and usually seen in winter plumage (as shown). In summer whole head, neck, and upper breast become dark. HABITS; Much as other auks, though better at taking off from water. MAY BE CONFUSED with juveniles of 238, 239, 242.

242 Puffin, *Fratercula arctica.* Resident; widespread colonies, except south-east England, on islands and cliffs with fissures, boulders, scree, and, most commonly, turfy slopes. Off-shore in winter; may be blown inland by storms. DESCRIPTION: 12 inches. Sexes alike. Big, parrot-like bill, duller in winter, and much smaller in dark-faced juvenile. VOICE: Low-pitched growl used at all times. HABITS: Much as other auks. Splayed feet noticeable in flight when near landing. Looks very compact and buoyant on water. Walks quite well on land with rolling gait. Usually social and breeds in huge colonies. MAY BE CONFUSED (juvenile) with 238, 239, 241.

RAIL OR CRAKE ORDER

Small-medium to large land and water birds, mainly residents and summer visitors. Sexes more or less alike. Plumage often brown. Legs and toes large, bodies curiously compressed-looking, very shy and secretive except for common aquatic species; others mainly marsh-birds with peculiar calls and 'songs'.

243 Corncrake, *Crex crex.* Summer visitor and passage migrant, breeds occasionally England, Wales, S. Scotland; widespread north Scotland, Ireland. Hayfields, rough pastures, bogs, and nettlebeds. DESCRIPTION: $10\frac{1}{2}$ inches. Sexes alike. Slender, narrow-bodied bird with longish legs. Winter and juvenile plumages lack greyish tint. VOICE: Repeated *kerreck kerreck*, grating and with great carrying power, is unmistakable call of male. HABITS: Extremely secretive, very seldom showing itself and then stalking furtively with head forward. If flushed, flies heavily with legs hanging. Presence usually made known by crekking of male. MAY BE CONFUSED with 244, 245.

244 **Spotted Crake,** *Porzana porzana.* Rare passage migrant and winter visitor, also probably breeding sporadically, even regularly, in widely separated areas, in bogs, marshes, and fens. DESCRIPTION: 9 inches. Sexes much alike. Like small 243 in shape. Female, winter and juvenile plumages duller than male. VOICE: Double ticking call, usually heard at night, is evidently equivalent to the crekking of 243. HABITS: Very secretive, but may appear in open at dusk, walking carefully and flirting tail like 246. Flies as 243. MAY BE CONFUSED with 243, 245, and with rarer small crakes.

245 **Water Rail,** *Rallus aquaticus.* Resident. winter visitor and passage migrant in reed-beds, fens, bogs, and tall wet vegetation of all kinds. DESCRIPTION: 11 inches. Sexes alike. Only long-billed rail or crake. VOICE: Most characteristic call is 'sharming': a grunt which ends as a squeal or scream and may be repeated many times, especially at night; also mammal-like squeal of alarm. HABITS: Much as 243 and 244; tail flirted like 246. Swims when necessary. MAY BE CONFUSED with 243, 244, juvenile 246.

246 **Moorhen,** *Gallinula chloropus.* Resident and winter visitor, local north Scotland. Near all types of water except fast-flowing mountain streams. DESCRIPTION: 13 inches. Sexes alike. A rather narrow-looking bird with cocked tail, generally dark in plumage with conspicuous white under tail. Juveniles dark brown with whitish throats, obscure marks on flanks and larger whitish area under tail. VOICE: Well-known call is rather harsh *perr-uck*, which has several variants. Repeated loud notes uttered when fighting. HABITS: Characteristic swimming action with head jerking forward as though it were a great effort. Walks carefully with head down and cocked tail, running to take heavy flight with hanging legs. Often perches

in trees and bushes. MAY BE CONFUSED with 247, and (juveniles) with 245.

247 **Coot,** *Fulica atra.* Resident and winter visitor, rare north Scotland. Sheets of water with reed-beds and other cover; broad rivers. In winter on open waters, sometimes on sea or estuaries. DESCRIPTION: 15 inches. Sexes alike. Bigger and much stouter than 246. Narrow white bar on wing in flight. Juvenile much browner with whitish breast and throat, no white frontal shield and yellowish bill. VOICE: Usual note single loud creaking call resembling 246 but easily distinguished. HABITS: Rather squat tail-less shape on water, but looks quite elongated in flight owing to stretched legs. Feeds by diving, but comes to shore to graze, walking like 246. Large flocks may form in winter. MAY BE CONFUSED with 246, juveniles with 170.

GAME-BIRD ORDER

Wild relatives of domesticated poultry. Mainly resident (several introduced) and sedentary. Sexes usually distinct with males much larger and more conspicuous. Bare areas of skin (wattles) on head. Rather social outside breeding season. Mainly vegetable feeders: grain shoots. Wings conspicuously convex in rapid beating flight.

248 **Capercaillie,** *Tetrao urogallus.* Resident (re-introduced) in Scotland from Stirlingshire to south-east Sutherland. Coniferous and mixed woodland, especially with birches. DESCRIPTION: Male 33–35, female 23–25 inches. Sexes differ. Juvenile resembles female. VOICE: Male has remarkable rhythmic 'song' of regular form, with fizzing and popping noises, which he utters when defending territory; female has hollow-sounding *kok* call like 252. HABITS: Flies with series of quick beats followed by glide and can steer easily through trees. Walks and runs on ground where it feeds; also perches to eat shoots and to roost. Singly, in family coveys or in small parties of separate sexes. MAY BE CONFUSED with 249.

249 **Black Grouse,** *Lyrurus tetrix.* Resident, very local north and west England and Wales; local in Scotland; on moorland edge, including birch woods and young conifers. DESCRIPTION: Male 20–22, female 16–17 inches. Sexes differ. Male distinguished from 248 by size and by white under lyre-shaped

tail. Female brown, paler than 250, less boldly marked than 248, with white wing-bar and distinctly forked tail. VOICE: Male's song called descriptively 'rookooing'; also wheezing call at the communal leks or displaying grounds. Female has double call like 248. HABITS: Flies and walks much as 248. Famous for communal displays by males with females in attendance, usually on grassy patches called leks. Roosts chiefly on ground. Packs form after breeding season. MAY BE CONFUSED with 248 and (female) with 250.

250 **Red Grouse,** *Lagopus lagopus scoticus.* Resident, local to common on heather moorland in west and north Britain, Ireland (distinct race), and larger islands. Now considered by most authorities to be race of European **Willow Grouse,** *Lagopus lagopus.* DESCRIPTION: 13–15½ inches, males somewhat larger. Sexes rather alike. Male redder in winter, paler in summer; winter female like summer male and even yellower in summer.

Juvenile at first resembles summer female. VOICE: Usual call is well-known *Go-back go-back go-back* which also forms part of male's song. HABITS: Much as other game-birds, flying low and hard. Males prominent in spring, but for much of the year birds hard to see unless flushed. Packs form when family parties link up. MAY BE CONFUSED with 251 and with female 248, 249.

251 **Ptarmigan,** *Lagopus mutus.* Resident in Scottish Highlands on bare mountain-tops. DESCRIPTION: 13–14 inches. Sexes rather alike. In summer male beautifully mottled grey and yellow with black and white imposed; outer part of wings white and underparts white. Female lacks grey tone and looks almost golden brown. In autumn male loses yellowish tone and becomes grey; female becomes much greyer. In winter both pure white, except for very short black tail and area round eye in male. VOICE: Usual call grating *gwark*; also explosive song by male. HABITS: Much like 250 but owing to bare habitat, tends to crouch low in open and is very difficult to see. Packs form in autumn. MAY BE CONFUSED (in summer) with 250.

252 **Pheasant,** *Phasianus colchicus.* Introduced resident, widespread to general except north Scotland, some parts of Ireland, and some islands. Agricultural land with small woods; riverside fields and marshes; scrubwoods and parks. DESCRIPTION:

Male 30–35 (tail up to 20), female 21–25 inches (tail may be 8). Sexes differ; male's plumage varies considerably; flight feathers paler brown than body. Females and juveniles much less conspicuous. VOICE: Usual call or crow of male loud *kok kok* which may be repeated many times. Female generally silent. HABITS: Upright stance of male well-known from countless paintings; female crouches much more, but both run with heads up. Flight of rapid beats is only sprint and cannot be sustained. Though obvious enough in winter, Pheasants are hard to see in summer except when flushed. MAY BE CONFUSED (juveniles) with 253–5.

253 **Quail,** *Coturnix coturnix*. Scarce summer visitor to southeastern England, sporadic elsewhere. Mainly corn-crops, but also in hay and clover. DESCRIPTION: 7 inches. Sexes nearly alike. Smallest game-bird. VOICE: Liquid 'wet-my-lips' call of male usual indication of presence. HABITS: Very rarely seen. Runs and flies like other game-birds but is difficult to flush. MAY BE CONFUSED with young of 252, 254, 255.

254 **Partridge,** *Perdix perdix*. Resident in agricultural land, except north Scotland and parts of Ireland. DESCRIPTION: 12 inches. Sexes nearly alike. Very rounded game-bird with short reddish-brown tail. Male's horseshoe on lower breast absent or poorly shown by most females. Juvenile lacks orange-brown and chestnut adornments. VOICE: Grating *kir-rick kir-rick* is usual call. HABITS: Usually in pairs or coveys scurrying over fields or feeding quietly when not alarmed. Flies quite readily in game-bird style. Seldom perches off ground. MAY BE CONFUSED with 255, or young 252, or its young with 253.

255 **Red-legged Partridge,** *Alectoris rufa*. Introduced resident in south and east England, local to absent elsewhere; on drier agricultural land, downs, sand dunes, and brecks. DESCRIPTION: 13½ inches. Sexes alike. Rather larger than 254 with less rounded back and longer tail. Juvenile lacks adornments of underparts and looks very like 254. VOICE: Male's song is repeated *chuckchuckah*; also a double *chuck chuck* of alarm. HABITS: Runs much more than 254 and is reluctant to fly; otherwise very similar. MAY BE CONFUSED with 254 and with young 252, or its young with 253.

ADDITION TO PIGEON ORDER

256 **Collared Dove,** *Streptopelia decaocto*. First identified breeding in Norfolk, 1956. Now widespread resident all over Britain, including many islands, and Ireland. Usually near houses and farms, especially with conifers and chicken-runs. DESCRIPTION: 11 inches. Sexes alike. Distinguished from 181 by narrower white-edged black half-collar and by more uniform upper parts, but especially by more white and less black on underside of tail. Confusion much easier with domesticated Barbary Doves which often fly free. Collared Dove is greyer above with main flight feathers almost black rather than dark brown. Juveniles, darker than adults, have faint collar. VOICE: Penetrating triple coo: *hoo-hoo hoo* with emphasis on second note, quite different from purr of 181, while Barbary Dove emphasizes first note. Also a loud mewing call in flight or when alighting. HABITS: Walks rather heavily on ground, and will feed with chickens, sparrows and other birds, though remaining rather wary. MAY BE CONFUSED with 181 and Barbary Dove.

FLIGHT SKETCHES OF DUCKS

♀ and ♂

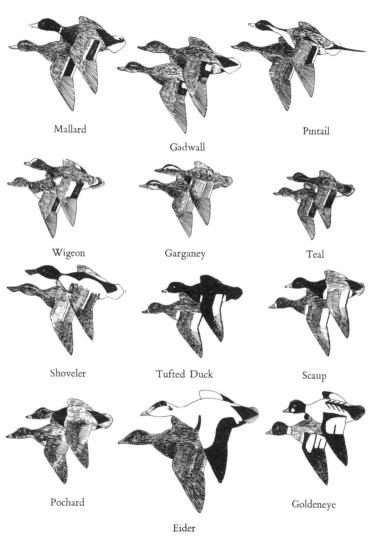

Mallard

Gadwall

Pintail

Wigeon

Garganey

Teal

Shoveler

Tufted Duck

Scaup

Pochard

Eider

Goldeneye

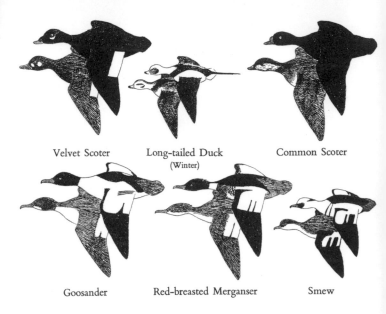

Velvet Scoter

Long-tailed Duck
(Winter)

Common Scoter

Goosander

Red-breasted Merganser

Smew

BIRDS OF PREY IN FLIGHT

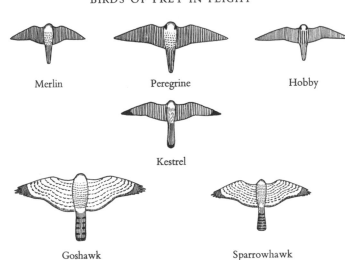

Merlin

Peregrine

Hobby

Kestrel

Goshawk

Sparrowhawk

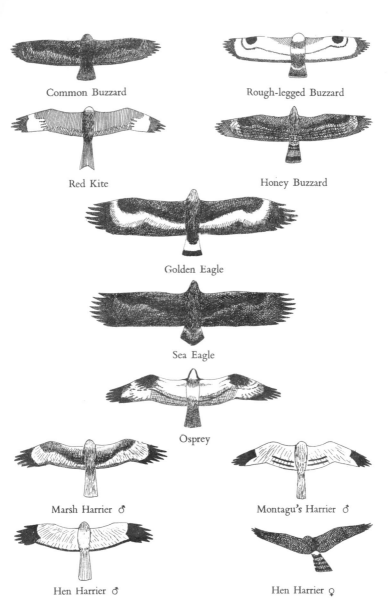

Common Buzzard

Rough-legged Buzzard

Red Kite

Honey Buzzard

Golden Eagle

Sea Eagle

Osprey

Marsh Harrier ♂

Montagu's Harrier ♂

Hen Harrier ♂

Hen Harrier ♀

BOOKS TO READ

The principal works of reference are the *Handbook of British Birds* by H.F. Witherby and others (London: Witherby, 5 volumes), and *Birds of the British Isles* by D. A. Bannerman and G. E. Lodge (Edinburgh: Oliver and Boyd), 12 volumes. Other books on British birds, covering their identification, life histories, and study, are:

Watching Birds by James Fisher (Penguin)

Bird Spotting by John Holland (Blandford)

Birds' Eggs and Nesting Habitats by Siegfried Hoeher, edited by Winwood Reade (Blandford)

A New Dictionary of Birds edited by Sir A. Landsborough Thomson (Nelson)

The Oxford Book of Birds by Bruce Campbell and Donald Watson (O.U.P.)

Nesting Birds, Eggs and Fledglings by Winwood Reade and Eric Hosking (Blandford)

Index of Scientific Names

INDEX OF SCIENTIFIC NAMES

INDEX OF SCIENTIFIC NAMES

Index of English Names

(The numbers are those of the illustrations and corresponding descriptive paragraphs in the text)

INDEX OF ENGLISH NAMES

INDEX OF ENGLISH NAMES